WHERE HE STANDS

WHERE HE STANDS

The Life and Convictions of
Spiro T. Agnew

with an introduction by
Richard M. Nixon

Hawthorn Books, Inc.
Publishers
New York

First Edition: 1968

PUBLISHER'S PREFACE

"What do you know about Spiro T. Agnew?" I was asked at Miami . . . Chicago . . . Interlochen, Michigan . . . London, England . . . Edinburgh, Scotland, and . . . Salzburg, Austria. For I was an Illinois Alternate Delegate-at-Large to the Republican National Convention before I left for Europe after a day in Chicago and two days in the National Music Camp.

Now . . . *Spiro T. Agnew is a household name.* For he was brought into the limelight through the marvel of modern communication media as the vice presidential nominee of the Republican Party.

But what kind of a man is he . . . what are his basic philosophies . . . what has he done . . . where does he stand on the major issues with which America is faced? In this book you will find the answers. For the answers to these questions are what people wanted to know when they asked: "What do you know about Agnew?" . . . the question that motivated the publishing of this book.

And as you read *Where He Stands,* you will realize the wisdom of Richard Nixon in selecting Governor Agnew as his running mate. For he was searching for a man of action who could meet the challenges of change with the right mental attitude . . . an emotionally mature individual who could perceive the necessity to lay the foundations to prevent in the future the difficulties of the past and the present.

Also as you read *Where He Stands,* you will see how Spiro Agnew, the son of a Greek immigrant who was not too proud to earn an honest livelihood peddling vegetables on the streets of Baltimore during the Depression years, helped his father while attending school. His life experience is a true modern Horatio Alger story.

As you read, you will understand why Spiro Agnew was a good son, is a good husband . . . father and . . . citizen. You will like the Agnew family. It is truly American in the most desirable sense.

In Governor Agnew's speech in which he nominated Richard Nixon for the presidency of the United States, he said:

> *When a nation is in crisis and when history speaks firmly to that nation that it needs a man to match the times—you don't create such a man; you don't discover such a man; you recognize such a man.*

And when you read through *Where He Stands,* you will recognize a man qualified to become the Vice President of the United States of America and . . . a good team worker for the man he nominated for the presidency . . . Richard Nixon.

W. CLEMENT STONE

Contents

WHERE HE STANDS

WHY I CHOSE TED AGNEW

by Richard M. Nixon

Before I recommended that the Republican National Convention select Spiro (Ted) Agnew to be the Republican nominee for Vice President, I consulted more than a hundred leading Republicans whose judgment I respected. I seriously considered more than a dozen very able men, all of whom were of presidential and vice presidential caliber. In the end, I selected Ted Agnew as the one who best met my exacting criteria:

Qualified to be President;
An effective campaigner;
An administrator who could assume new responsibilities for the office of Vice President.

My primary concern was to select a man who had the courage, the character and the intellect not only to be Vice President, but also to be an effective President if the need arose.

I know Ted Agnew well. We have had long and tough discussions. We have examined each other's ideas, debated issues and tested each other. He has real depth and genuine warmth. Having watched his performance as Governor of Maryland for two years, I was deeply impressed by his tremendous brain power, great courage and unprejudiced legal mind. He has vigor and imagination and, above all, he acts.

1

Under pressure, he is poised and controlled. When it comes to carrying the ball and resisting the attack, he's got it.

Ted has come through the fire. He has experienced poverty and prejudice and risen above them on his own merits. He has experienced war—out front with Patton's armored division in World War II. He stood up to counterattack at the Battle of the Bulge. Recalled, he served his country in the armed forces a second time, during the Korean War. He now is undergoing the fire that all parents experience whose sons are in the front lines of Vietnam. As a champion of social and racial justice, he has experienced the fire of reverses in local politics, only to be vindicated by the voters and returned to ever higher office.

There is a quiet confidence about him. In this atomic age, the President is constantly facing the threat of nuclear war. Ted Agnew is the one in whom I would have confidence to face that threat.

In addition to his personal qualities, Ted Agnew has established that his thinking is broadly representative of the mainstream both within the Republican Party and within the nation as a whole. We have got to get the country together. We must rebuild the unity of the party as a first step to rebuilding national unity. We must move both the party and the country toward the political center. Ted Agnew has national, not sectional, views. He is a national, not a regional, candidate. He has constantly sought reconciliation between civil rights for the minority and civil rights for the majority. He has said: "Racial discrimination, unequal education and job opportunities must be eliminated no matter whom that displeases—but anarchy, rioting or civil disobedience has no constructive purpose in our constitutional republic." He has also said: "The old, the sick and the poor must be tended. We must build independence and pride in the Negro community—make black Americans partners." I—and I believe most Republicans and most Americans—agree.

We must build bridges to human dignity across the gulf which today separates black America from white America.

Black Americans do not want more government programs which perpetuate dependency. They do not want to be a colony within a nation. They want the pride, the self-respect and the dignity that can come only if they have an equal chance to own their own homes, their own businesses, to be managers and executives as well as workers.

Ted Agnew's record as an innovative governor of a border state proves that he will contribute greatly in the development of new programs to provide all the underprivileged—irrespective of color—with that equal chance. Maryland is a small state but it has been called "America in miniature." It has urban, suburban and rural problems. It has industry and farming. It has those who believe in the politics of the far right, the far left and everywhere in between. As a border state, it has all aspects of the problems that surround the relationships between black and white Americans. Most of all, Maryland is experiencing rapid and far-reaching change.

Governor Agnew has given Maryland a vigorous, imaginative and, above all, an action government. The antiquated fiscal structure was reformed providing tax breaks for the elderly and lower-income families. The state's national ranking in public education leaped from twelfth to fifth place as a result of the Agnew policies, which, for the first time, granted state aid for kindergartens and inner-city schools and increased teachers' salaries throughout the school and college system. The Agnew Administration was the first in America to provide state funds to improve local law-enforcement efforts. Its programs to abate air and water pollution have been hailed as models for the nation.

The Agnew record in behalf of civil rights stands as an example to public officials everywhere. As the chief executive of Maryland's largest county, before he was elected governor, he sponsored one of the nation's first public-accommodations laws. As Governor of Maryland he set a series of precedents: the first Fair Housing Bill enacted south of the Mason-Dixon line, the first Governor's Code of Fair Practices to guarantee equal employment within the state government, the repeal of

3

the state's antimiscegenation law, and the appointment of Negroes to responsible governmental positions.

At the same time, he has drawn a sharp distinction between civil rights and civil disorder. He is a staunch believer that government must not yield to threats, whether from mobs in the street or on a college campus, and he has demonstrated this conviction in actions as well as words. He stood firm against a threatened student insurrection, and he has moved swiftly to put down civil disorder, holding there can be no progress without respect for the law. "Capitulation to violence, either to keep the peace or from misguided compassion, is suicidal for society," he has said. "If we reward violence, violence will soon supplant law as the accepted instrument to achieve social change. Yet if we deny just grievances exist, we destroy society just as surely."

From the political point of view, one reason that I chose Ted Agnew as my running mate is that he has shown himself to be an effective campaigner. In 1962, when he ran for the post of Baltimore County Executive, he was easily elected even though the county is overwhelmingly Democratic. In 1966, seeking the Republican gubernatorial nomination, he waged an aggressive primary campaign and easily defeated four opponents, winning 83 percent of the vote. He continued his effective campaign against his Democratic opponents and rescued Maryland from the leadership of a Democrat committed to segregation. He did this only two years after George Wallace, running in a presidential primary, had demonstrated how greatly disposed Maryland was to the old pattern. Ted Agnew won with a plurality of 81,775 to become the fifth Republican governor in Maryland's 180 years of statehood—in a state where the registered Democrats outnumber the registered Republicans by more than 3 to 1.

Ted Agnew's campaign style is direct and honest. He is articulate; he is good on dialogue; he does not lose his cool. He has an ability to make listeners consider the issues. His fairness, logic and common sense appeal to people. He has a history of having won support from Independents and Demo-

4

crats. He is a hard worker, dedicated to work for Republican candidates throughout the country. He has good health and stamina, drive and ambition. He will campaign in a way that will not jeopardize our ability to unite the country and give truly national leadership in the years ahead.

In part, I picked Ted Agnew to be my Vice President because he is the man who can best work with me. I believe we will make an effective team. We trust each other, communicate easily; our approach is similar, our backgrounds complementary. My main experience has been at the federal level—in the House of Representatives, the Senate and eight years as Vice President under that great Republican and great President, General Eisenhower. I have long been concerned with the problems of foreign affairs and traveled abroad widely, seeing the various faces of Communism from Caracas to Moscow, seeing the progress of Europe and Japan, seeing the struggles of the less developed areas overwhelmed by poverty, disease and instability.

Ted Agnew, on the other hand, has long experience at the local and state levels of government. He has proved himself an effective administrator, a Republican executive who can be effective even with a Democratic legislature. He knows from firsthand experience that the proliferation of overlapping federal programs has achieved little because of bureaucratic disorder and competition between various levels of government that only inhibit state legislatures in acting intelligently and without rancor on city problems.

I will ask him, as Vice President, to assume responsibility for the development of more effective partnership between all levels of government in seeking solutions to our many domestic problems. There must be a better way than the way the Democrats are doing it now—bigger and bigger federal government spending more and more and accomplishing less and less. Ted Agnew is well qualified to spearhead the building of an effective and clear division of responsibility and authority between all the levels of government. Having served on the nine-member Executive Committee of the national Governors' Conference and on the President's Advisory Commission on Intergovernmental Relations, he will provide an effective link with all the governors of the states with whom he has developed a good working relationship. Together we must develop a new system in which each citizen can feel effective, can know that he has a contribution to make that is needed, and at the same time can feel that the system can help him effectively when he is in trouble. A system of compassion, of justice, of law.

Another very important asset that Ted Agnew brings to the vice presidency must not be overlooked. He is an experienced and effective labor-relations lawyer. He has demonstrated his ability to bring the parties of a dispute together. Both labor and management have publicly given him credit for the settlement of a long tugboat strike in Baltimore within the first few weeks of his term as governor. I will ask him as Vice President to be my chief mediator in jurisdictional disputes—between federal and state governments, between the executive and legislative branches, within the various departments of the federal government. I will ask him to help me and my cabinet in mediating disruptive strikes that seriously endanger the strength of the nation.

Of course, there is no training that alone can prepare any man to be President or Vice President. If the man has the inner character, ability and dedication he will grow in the office. Ted Agnew has demonstrated that he has the attributes of a statesman of the first rank. He has the qualities of intellect, the will, the imaginative capacity to be simultaneously compassionate and decisive. He is a team player, calm under fire, a pragmatic administrator who strives toward the ideal goals of justice, harmony, equality and tranquility.

I am proud to have Ted Agnew as my running mate. I know that the people of the United States will be proud to have him as their Vice President.

THE BUILDING OF A MAN: A Biography

by Ann Pinchot

"There can be a mystique about a man," Richard Nixon said recently. "You can look him in the eye and know he's got it. This guy has got it."

He was speaking of Spiro T. Agnew, the man he had chosen as his running mate on the Republican presidential ticket. Mr. Nixon felt that three qualifications were essential in the man who would be his choice for Vice-President: the leadership ability to assume the presidency, if that emergency arose; a deep understanding of domestic affairs and the problems of the counties and cities; and the spirit to wage a good campaign.

In recent years, when many would dismiss the basic virtues of our forefathers as "square," Mr. Nixon praised Spiro Agnew as "basically an old-fashioned patriot."

In his background and upbringing, Spiro T. Agnew represents the heart of America, the second-generation American raised with an appreciation for what America has to offer its citizens and how to use its democratic processes for self-advancement.

Agnew's father was born in Greece in the small rocky village of Gargalianoi, Messenia, in the southeastern Peloponnesus. The family name was originally Anagnostopoulos, which Spiro's father shortened to Anagnost when he emigrated to the United States. Later, it was simplified to Agnew.

When he arrived in Boston in 1897, the senior Agnew

7

found his first job as a barber. It took only one irate customer to convince the employer that his young apprentice had more ambition than experience. Through hard work, it was not long before he acquired his own restaurant and later one in Schenectady, New York. Eventually he moved to Baltimore.

In Baltimore, the senior Agnew opened a restaurant on Howard Street called the Brighton. He later operated and owned the Piccadilly Restaurant on the same street. Theodore S. Agnew became a leader in Baltimore's Greek community in his late thirties. He married an attractive young American woman, the former Margaret Akers of Bristol, Virginia. She was the widow of Dr. William R. Pollard, a prominent veterinarian, and had a young son, W. Roy, eleven years older than Spiro.

Spiro was born on November 9, 1918, and spent his boyhood in a friendly, comfortable house in Forest Park. He grew up in the post-World War I years, when America was changing from a rural to an industrial culture, but his boyhood was spent secure in the warm, comfortable ways of American family life. He was a tall youngster with the well-shaped head and strong classic nose that marked his Greek ancestors. A snapshot of him, which his wife Judy treasures, shows a ten-year-old boy, his hair neatly parted, wearing a white shirt with a neatly tied necktie, his arm on his canine friend of questionable ancestry, Friskey.

Agnew never learned to speak Greek, and the only time he remembers hearing it spoken was when his father was on the telephone with a Greek compatriot or when Greek friends came to visit. He regrets not having learned the language, but the Greek heritage, with its reverence for the principles of democracy and its emphasis on wisdom, reason, and justice, remains ever with him.

In the nation's earlier years, candidates for office usually came from a self-educated, log-cabin background. More recently, it is the third-generation millionaire with unlimited resources at his command who seeks public office. But Spiro T. Agnew has gone through the experiences of many Americans

The Agnew family album shows Agnew in uniform, 1942. (*Wide World*)

in the past years, and as a result he understands their problems. During the Depression his father not only lost his restaurant, but could find no work to provide for his family. Finally, he hired a truck, got up at three each morning to buy produce at the wholesale markets, and sold vegetables to friends who had not lost their businesses. After school, his son helped him. But the elder Agnew insisted that the boy continue his schooling—a respect for education that Spiro Agnew inherited and that has inspired him to hammer home to today's school dropouts that knowledge is power.

The Governor remembers his father saying, "It's not how intelligent you are, but how much you apply yourself and discipline your thinking." His father often spoke before local groups and enlisted the help of fourteen-year-old Spiro in preparing his talks. "I can still see him," the Governor recalls. "He'd give me the ideas and then add, 'You can say this better than I can. Write it out for me.'" While the Governor's best subject was English, this is how he learned to perfect and polish the eloquence and clarity for which he is now known.

Spiro was a conscientious student in the Baltimore local schools. He graduated in February, 1937, and immediately entered Johns Hopkins University to study chemistry.

Times were difficult and confused, with the threat of war in Europe. "We felt as though we had no roots and didn't know what was going to happen to us." As a result, his scholastic concentration in sophomore year began to decline and he was distracted by other things than school. "My father became a little unhappy over this. Hopkins was not an inexpensive school and he was not a man of affluence. He was dismayed at how little attention I was paying to my studies. I went into my third year less and less interested. Finally, my father said he couldn't keep me in Hopkins any longer and perhaps it would do me a lot of good to get out and get a job to pay for my education." Agnew left Hopkins just after he decided to become a lawyer and found work in the file room of the Maryland Casualty Company. Since jobs were hard to come by in those years, his first pay was eleven dollars a week.

He enrolled at the University of Baltimore Law School, attending night classes and working by day for the Maryland Casualty Company, where he met his future wife.

She was Elinor Isabel Judefind, pretty, slender, and dark-eyed, the daughter of Dr. W. Lee Judefind, a chemist and executive of the Davison Chemical Company. "Spiro says he tripped over me in the file room," she says of their first meeting. "Judy and I grew up within four blocks of each other and didn't know it until we met at work," says the Governor.

On their first date, says Mrs. Agnew, who is called Judy by her family and friends, they went to the movies and then had chocolate milk shakes at a drive-in stand. Their courtship was a round of movies, bowling, and double-dating with other young couples and meeting in various homes for suppers and good talk. Spiro had little time between his work and law classes, but it was soon evident that they were right for each other. "Shortly after our meeting," he says, "I was taken out of the file room and given a job as assistant underwriter in the Sprinkler Leakage and Water Damage Department. I got an office and a secretary and thirteen dollars a week. By the time I went into service, I was earning eighteen dollars a week. I went through a year of law school and still wasn't doing anything scholastically. The war was becoming more complex and the draft more imminent. I was cutting a lot of classes. I still didn't have anything to get married on." Five months later, in April, 1941, their engagement was announced. They hoped to marry before Spiro went into the service, but he was drafted in September at twenty-one dollars a month—not exactly a marrying income. He was selected for Officer Candidate School. Like many other young couples, they waited, and three days after Spiro graduated as a second lieutenant from the Fort Knox, Kentucky, OCS, and eighteen months after their first date, they were married.

At Fort Knox, Judy Agnew remembers, their first homes were a series of cabins, but finally they were fortunate enough to find quarters over a garage in Elizabeth Town, and here they set up their first housekeeping. They were so proud of

11

that little apartment, but not for long; shortly afterward, Spiro was transferred to Camp Campbell in Kentucky and the search for living space began again. But now, Judy remained with her young husband only until May. She was expecting their first child, and she went to her family in Baltimore to spend the last two months before the baby's birth. Spiro hoped to take Judy and the child, Pamela Lee, back to camp with him, but was advised against it, as he was scheduled to report to Fort Meade, Maryland.

While Spiro served in Europe as a company commander of the 10th Armored Division, Judy and baby Pam lived with the Judefinds. Lieutenant Agnew served in four separate campaigns in Europe. The heaviest fighting he saw was at Ilshofen.

After demobilization, the Governor recalls, "I returned immediately to law school, for now I had an insatiable desire to learn and get on with my education. I had much better scholastic ability than before and, of course, greater incentive, with a wife and children to support."

While studying at night, Spiro Agnew got a job with a law firm in downtown Baltimore, Smith and Barrett. Through George Oursler, a friend of his father's, he had met the senior partner, Michael Paul Smith, and become a law clerk. His pay was twenty-five dollars a week. From the On the Job Training under the G.I. Bill, he received another twenty-five dollars a week. But it was tough supporting a wife and two children— soon to be three—on that sum. His father helped during any emergencies, but the young Agnews were pretty short on money.

Their one-bedroom apartment grew overcrowded, after the birth of their second child, James Rand, and in 1946 the family moved to Baltimore County to their first real home, a comfortable house with living room, kitchen, and two bedrooms on one floor and two unfinished rooms above. They lived here until Spiro was recalled to service during the Korean conflict, when they sold the house and Judy and the children followed him to Fort Meade and from there to Fort Benning, Georgia, where he served for another year.

Spiro graduated from law school in 1947 while still working with Smith and Barrett. Once he had graduated, his G.I. assistance was cut off, and the law firm seemed unable to raise his salary to what he'd previously earned. So he made the decision to go out on his own.

He opened a law firm and failed miserably. He had no clients. All he had was overhead. Financially pressed, he took a job as a claims adjuster for an insurance company in Baltimore at a salary of three thousand a year. But at least he could support his family.

Then he found an ad in a newspaper for an assistant personnel director in a food market. "The salary was a hundred dollars a week, which seemed to me like all the money in the world," he says. Schreiber Brothers hired him, and he found it a challenging job, since his work covered many areas of the operation.

At that time, there was on the Board of Directors of Schreiber Brothers a man who was to influence Spiro Agnew's life greatly: Judge Herbert Moser. He and Judge Moser talked occasionally and the judge knew Spiro was eager to get back into law practice.

He recommended Spiro for a position with a big law firm and Spiro got the job. But it looked like a dead end, and after a year Spiro decided to go out on his own again.

Judge Moser found him a job with a research group for the Court of Appeals Rules Committee, "so I'd find some sustenance in part-time work," the Governor recalls. Again he opened a small office and, by hard effort, he managed to gross five thousand dollars the first year.

As a young lawyer, Agnew's reason and deliberation made a deep impression on both management and labor, and by virtue of his sense of fair play, he was in demand as a mediator. Later, after he entered public service, his deep personal interest helped to prevent crippling strikes.

His busy legal practice did not keep Agnew from sharing in his family's life. He was a conscientious and devoted father.

Pamela, the firstborn daughter, with her parents in 1943. (*Wide World*)

Sometimes, Judy Agnew says, she wondered how to juggle three children and the responsibilities of a home. "But my husband would pitch in when he came home from the office. He would bathe one child while I took care of the other. He was an expert at making formulas and he washed diapers. And if there was an emergency, he would get the meals, too. There were many times when I had to call him during that time, when I wasn't feeling well, and he would help right away."

Admitting cheerily that she "majored in marriage," Judy Agnew has found fulfillment in her husband and her family. Those who know her predict that the step from a warm, sensible, and efficient wife and mother to the helpmate of a vice-presidential candidate will be taken easily and with the good sense and lack of pretense that is characteristic of her.

The Agnews have four children, Pamela, twenty-five, Randy, twenty-two, Susan, twenty, and Kimberly, twelve. Like all families, they have had to mold their philosophy of child rearing to the demands of the times, but they stress the importance of respecting children as individuals, without being indulgent with them, and the family loyalties and virtues from both the Hellenic and Virginia ancestors.

When Agnew was elected Governor and they were obliged to move to Annapolis, Pamela was reluctant to accompany them. She decided to remain in Baltimore County, where she wanted to be close to her schoolteaching job. (Later she took a job in Baltimore City as a social worker.) Now, however, she expects to take a leave of absence from her job to work on her father's campaign.

Judy Agnew confesses to a natural reluctance to let her children go out on their own. "But they have been taught right from wrong, and fortified by a good sense of values, they should do well."

"Susan was our rebel," Mrs. Agnew continues, but with the tolerance one gives a child who has turned out well. "Except for Randy, our son, who decided in his second year of college to leave school. I guess he was suffering from the sophomore slump. Spiro reminded his son of how Albert

Einstein had once defined education as 'that which remains after you've forgotten everything you learned at school.' But that still meant Randy had to attend school and we insisted that he at least finish the year. Then Randy joined the Navy Reserve and was called up for service."

Petty Officer James Rand Agnew is a Navy Seabee in Vietnam, and presently his unit, Mobile Construction Battalion 8, is repairing a bridge in Hué blown up by Viet Cong sappers during the February 1968 offensive. Randy was in sick bay having his ears "unplugged" as the result of washing in the muddy river water when he heard of his father's nomination for the vice-presidency. His battalion is due for rotation back in the States in October, when he is hopeful of doing a little campaigning for his father. Now, after his war experience, Randy is eager to come home and continue his schooling. His wife, Ann, is still too young to cast a ballot for her father-in-law. Their child, one-year-old Michelle Ann, has a distinguished and loving babysitter in Grandmother Agnew. After the convention in Miami Beach, Judy Agnew, suffering from hay fever and a virus, went to Ocean City, Maryland, for a brief rest. Here she was joined by Ann and Michelle Ann, and all of her press appointments were arranged to take place while the baby was sleeping.

Susan, who is now twenty and a secretary at Westinghouse, lives at home with the family. Her sense of rebellion was tempered with the rational thinking that distinguishes her father, and the relationship between parents and daughter is solid and warm.

Sometimes Judy Agnew worries because their youngest child, daughter Kimberly, may not be getting all the parental attention she needs. But after all, she consoles herself, it is the quality of affection not the quantity that matters. After the convention, the Agnews telephoned the good news to Kimberly.

"Is that so," she said politely, but quite unimpressed.

"That's the reaction of a twelve-year-old," Judy Agnew said laughingly.

Agnew (left) as an army lieutenant in 1943. (*Wide World*)

Kimberly is starting eighth grade in an accelerated course, and Mrs. Agnew feels that the youngster will need her during the school term. Fortunately, the housekeeper at the Governor's Mansion is a wonderful woman whose contribution to the campaign will be to look after Kim's needs. And, of course, even when she is campaigning with the Governor, Judy Agnew will keep in close touch with her children.

Childbearing and the years have added a few pounds to Judy Agnew, but she accepts them with a wry equanimity. At 5 feet 4 inches, she weighs 140 pounds and finds dieting a bore. She eats sparingly at lunch, perhaps a chicken sandwich, and when there were fewer demands on her time she belonged to the "Swim and Slim" classes at the Y.W.C.A. Dieting would probably be a lot easier if the Governor didn't enjoy her excellent spaghetti and if they didn't mark celebrations with spicy pizza. The Governor is also fond of avgolemino, a Greek chicken lemon soup, which unfortunately Judy never learned to make.

Agnew plays golf when he can and usually has a healthy tan. The Governor enjoys playing pool with his staff, but the time he can give to recreation is diminishing.

The seed of Spiro Agnew's public service took root, curiously enough, out of his interests as a family man. As part of her role as wife and mother, Judy also took an interest in those organizations that are part of middle-class family life. She became a board member of the Women's Civic League; is past president of the Ki-Wives, the womens auxiliary of the Kiwanis Club; and is a member of the Federation of Republican Women and a former Girl Scout leader. Spiro held no elective office, other than being president of the local Parent Teachers Association, until 1962. However, as a practicing attorney in Baltimore County and president of the Loch Raven Community Council, he had been active in moves to obtain open-spaces legislation in the county and in the successful drive for a Home Rule charter, under which the Board

Judy Agnew in the mid-1940s. (*Wide World*)

of County Commissioners was replaced with a full-time County Executive and Council in 1957.

In that year, Spiro T. Agnew was appointed minority member of the County Board of Appeals, which hears zoning appeals, and later became its chairman. His ouster in 1961 by the Democratic-controlled County Council, despite widespread backing from civic organizations, brought his name to new prominence. The following year he ran for County Executive. He won, despite a Democratic registration edge of nearly four to one.

Under his administration, Baltimore County became one of the first in the nation to enact a public accommodation law. His administration also built many new schools, improved teachers' salaries, reduced the pupil-teacher ratio by 14 percent, began public kindergartens, reorganized the police bureau, and pioneered in community college curricula to fill employment gaps in the fields of police work and social services.

During his first year in office, he was elected a director of the National Association of Counties and subsequently represented the association at congressional hearings.

In 1966, with the full endorsement of the Maryland Republican leaders, Agnew ran for Governor of the state of Maryland. Republicans and Democrats alike were impressed with his accomplishments. Without fanfare, working quietly and efficiently, this pragmatic young lawyer represented the new breed in American public life. He won the primary, and on November 8, 1966, the day before his forty-eighth birthday, Spiro T. Agnew was elected governor. In a three-way race, he had a margin of 81,775 votes over his Democratic opponent, George Mahoney, a segregationist.

The qualities in Spiro Agnew that his wife suggested had made him a good father—understanding, reason, fair play —were also the qualities that made him a good governor. Asked about her husband's character, Mrs. Agnew said with quiet pride, "He's a good administrator. He has brains, he's intelligent, and he has the ability to listen to reason. He's very

By 1948 the Agnews had three children and a German shepherd.
(*Wide World*)

conscientious. Once he's made up his mind to what he thinks is right, he stands by what he says. But if someone has a different view, he won't shut his ears to what the person may have to say."

In his inaugural address, Governor Agnew said in part: "If this day brings special promise, it is because we refuse to accept as inevitable things as they are or things as they have been. While it is indeed true that poverty does exist in times of prosperity, that ignorance does persist in an age of enlightenment, it is in the minds of men to deplore these imperfections and in the will of men to pursue the ideal.

"This is a time of vast and ever-accelerating change . . . a time probably representing the most difficult period in our growth since this country moved out of its totally rural years and into the incredibly complex areas of mass production and urbanization. This change, if order is to prevail, cannot go unguided. . . .

"It is within our power today to create a working, imaginative state government. Our role is vital and immediate. We must recognize that the benefits of legislative and administrative reform are dependent on a searching examination and dynamic revision of our total fiscal structure. There is little question that Maryland needs fiscal reform. There is little question that the executive branch of Maryland's state government needs to re-evaluate, revise, and reform many of its administrative functions and programs. . . . We must encourage this procedure by employing the soundest thinking of our most creative minds. And above all, we must generate an atmosphere in which that creativity can flourish. For it is the attitude that we bring to our labors that will determine the quality of our accomplishments. It is the way we think that must always determine the way we act. Once we are successful in improving the state of mind, we will surely be successful in improving the state of Maryland.

"I speak of a new state of mind, my fellow citizens, and if it should be given a name, let us call it the pursuit of excellence . . . which provides a discipline and a direction. . . .

Pamela, Randy and Susan with their father in 1953. (*Wide World*)

"We have seen great decisions of state become mired in the struggles of men to preserve personal power. And we are paying the price. Our cities, our air, and our waters reflect the price. And what tax-paying citizen will not willingly acknowledge that he, too, is paying the price.

"We pay for crime when we pay too little attention to its cures. We pay for pollution when we pay too little attention to its prevention. We pay for overcrowded schools when we fail to build new ones; for slums when we choose to ignore the onset of blight; for desperate and disillusioned human beings when we fail to encourage, educate, house, and employ them.

"It has become all too obvious that the cost of failure far exceeds the price of progress. It is evident that we can no longer tolerate from any elected official an attitude of how much can he promise, how little can he perform. It has become painfully clear that the reason we sometimes failed was that we were not, at all times, sincerely determined to succeed. . . .

"I call for a new spirit of leadership which will consciously and continually dedicate itself to the pursuit of excellence . . . All that I ask of others, I will demand of myself. For a people, not just a party, has elected me Governor. A people not just a party, sits in judgment. A people, not just a party, is waiting to be served. . . .

"A new day has come, bringing with it a new alliance which rejects tradition that fails to serve or inspire.

"This new alliance is not labeled conservative or liberal, rich or poor, white or black, Christian or Jew, Republican or Democrat. This new alliance should be called people . . . principle . . . progress. . . .

"Let us look at these challenging times of ours with the incisive realism that Christopher Fry looked at his, when he wrote:

> Dark and cold we may be, but this
> is not winter now. The frozen misery
> of centuries creaks, cracks, begins to move;
> The thunder is the thunder of the floes,

The whole family in 1957. (*Wide World*)

The thaw, the flood, the upstart Spring.
Thank God our time is now when wrong
Comes up to face us everywhere,
Never to leave us 'til we take
The longest stride of soul men ever took . . ."

For the Agnews, it was quite a change from their small comfortable house to the fifty-four-room, museum-like Governor's Mansion. But Judy Agnew is known for keeping her cool. To her housewife's eye, the Mansion needed not refurbishing but the application of fresh paint. The beautiful drapes had not been taken down and laundered since 1952. She kept all the drapes, carpets, and furniture. Except for the pieces that were recovered in two rooms, the major renovations were rewiring, new plumbing, heating, and air-conditioning. The Governor added a sauna bath to the restoration. But when the Mansion was spruced up, people got the impression that it had been completely redone.

For four months, while the work was in progress, the Agnews lived on the *Maryland Lady*, an 118-foot, ocean-going yacht owned by the state of Maryland. "We kept our own house for a little while," Judy Agnew says, "but then disposed of it. Another family has been living there since a year ago June. Spiro inherited a row house from his father, and his aunt lives there now."

While his father was living, Spiro often went to help him in business, for it was discovered that the elder Agnew was ill. No son could have been more thoughtful, Judy Agnew recalls, but he could help out only a short while, for the doctor insisted that the elder Agnew give up his business. Although stricken with cancer, Spiro's father lived for eight years and was eighty-six when he died.

Since her husband has been in public life, Mrs. Agnew's wardrobe has expanded. But she still prefers simple uncomplicated clothes of plain colors and good lines. She wore knits long before they became so popular because, she says, they are so comfortable and pack so easily. She buys "off the rack."

Three votes for Agnew!—Ted, Judy and daughter Pam. (*Wide World*)

But the Governor, who wears custom-made suits and shirts, often buys clothing for her in a variety of fabrics, either dresses or suits in a spectrum of colors. "His favorite color is orchid," she says, "yet oddly enough he's never bought me anything in that color." The rage over hemlines hasn't bothered her a bit; she wears her skirts to cover her knees.

The Governor has definite likes and dislikes in his choice of clothes, and Mrs. Agnew and the children have long given up even buying ties for him. But they do give him cuff links, which are a safe gift because he prefers French cuffs on his shirts. He frequently wears cuff links impressed with the state seal.

The Agnews entertain a good deal, but unless it is a state fuction they usually adjourn to the basement club room for Ping-pong, pocket billiards, or TV. They see a good deal of a small group of couples they knew when they were first married and who are known as the Saturday Night Group. The young wives first got together when their men were overseas. Their loyalties have remained strong, and they try to see one another at least once a month on a Saturday evening.

Agnew has great dignity and also a great respect for his office. He is a restrained and thoughtful man who loves people but has a natural aversion to the hoopla of American politics. He once said wrily that whenever he has a train of thought that requires concentration, "somebody wants me to stop and glorify National Pickle Week." Judy Agnew confesses that she is still too shy to wave to people.

Governor Agnew is religious in a private kind of way, and when he says grace, his wife says with gentle pride, there is always a freshness in his approach that guests find moving. An avid reader, he finds it difficult to keep up with books, since he must devote so much time to newspapers, magazines, and his own reading matter. But he is fond of history, is an avid admirer of Winston Churchill's works, and likes James Michener for his adroit blending of fact and fiction. He loves semiclassical music and has written poetry for his own pleasure (he rarely shares it with his family and staff). Although he

The happy winner in 1966 with his three women. (*Wide World*)

often presents an appearance of restraint, those who know him well find him a warm, genuinely likable person. He has a feeling for young people and has expressed his hopes for his children simply: he wants each of them to have a good education and a happy home life of their own.

When asked for her suggestions for a happy marriage, Judy Agnew says, "Patience and understanding, although there's not much difference between the two, is there? In our marriage, we have tried very hard to make each other happy."

When the Governor and Mrs. Agnew arrived in Miami Beach for the Republican Convention, they were not aware of the surprise in store for them. Spiro Agnew knew only that he would have the honor of making the address to nominate Richard M. Nixon for President of the United States. What he did not know was that not only Nixon but other influential leaders were aware of his admirable administration in Maryland.

For example, comprehensive fiscal reform was the first target of the Agnew administration, and with the support of Maryland's Democratic-controlled General Assembly, a thorough revision of the state's tax structure was enacted. The new bill established such innovations as a graduated income tax, tax credits for the elderly, a local-option income tax to provide local governments with an alternative revenue source to the property tax, state aid for local law enforcement agencies and kindergartens, and a special grant to inner city schools. As a result of the increased state aid to public schools, Maryland's educational ranking among the states moved from twelfth to fifth highest in the nation.

In the field of human rights, Spiro Agnew's administration sponsored the first statewide fair-housing bill enacted south of the Mason-Dixon Line. The century-old Anti-Miscegenation Law was repealed. Maryland's public accommodations statutes were extended to conform with federal legislation. Governor Agnew was the first Maryland governor to appoint a Negro to his personal staff and to issue a Governor's Code of Fair

Employment Practices outlawing discrimination in state service and in any firm doing business with the state.

As the result of administration-sponsored legislation, Maryland's highway construction programs were accelerated and state highway financing and planning procedures were completely revised. In addition, the administration gained legislative authorization to build three toll bridges across the Chesapeake Bay and a second tunnel beneath Baltimore Harbor. Maryland's first comprehensive highway-safety planning program was launched by Governor Agnew.

Maryland's waterways have received priority. After a year of planning, the Agnew administration introduced and won legislative approval of its Water Quality Control Program. The most massive and comprehensive such effort in state history, it is designed to combat and eventually eliminate all factors contributing to pollution.

Innovation and improvement within the executive branch of state government have been a major objective of the Agnew administration. The Governor's office was expanded to include five program executives operating under a cabinet-type arrangement to improve communication, coordination, and efficiency between the Governor's office and the more than 200 executive branch departments, agencies, boards, and commissions.

As a former County Executive, Governor Agnew keenly appreciates the importance of local governments. He was Maryland's first governor personally to tour each of the state's twenty-four subdivisions to meet with local leaders. Nearly 85 percent of the funds available under the fiscal reform program went into grants for local governments. The Agnew administration provided planning funds for rapid transit systems in both the Baltimore and Washington metropolitan areas. The state also purchased Baltimore's Friendship Airport in order to relieve the city of the financial burdens involved in its major capital improvement program and to ensure that the state had a major facility to accommodate the new super-jet service.

Randy Agnew training before he left for Vietnam. (*Wide World*)

Demonstrating the increased state responsibility for public safety, Governor Agnew established the Commission on Law Enforcement and the Administration of Justice to serve as a statewide crime-prevention planning unit.

Upon taking office, Governor Agnew faced a genuine crisis in Maryland's prisons. He moved to alleviate it through hiring of a new correctional chief, developing a new plan for state-local-regional prison ventures, and initiating unprecedented vocational rehabilitation efforts for inmates, completely funded by the federal government.

Maryland's economic development has surged ahead with assistance from such measures as a reform of the state business tax structure, which was developed in close cooperation with the state legislature.

Shortly after taking office, Governor Agnew was instrumental in settling Baltimore's lengthy tugboat strike and was credited by labor leaders with helping avoid a strike by food store clerks. Aware of the damaging trend toward public employee strikes, the Governor established the Committee on State-Labor Relations to develop effective guidelines.

On the national level, Governor Agnew has served on the Executive Committee of the National Governors Conference as vice-chairman of the conference's Committee on State-Urban Relations; as a member of the Republican Governors Association Campaign Committee; and as a member of the Republican Coordinating Committee Task Force on Federal, Fiscal, and Monetary Affairs. In July 1968, President Johnson appointed Governor Agnew to the Advisory Commission on Intergovernmental Relations.

As he delivered the address to nominate Richard M. Nixon for President, Governor Agnew spoke with warmth and conviction. For what Richard M. Nixon stood for, Spiro Theodore Agnew believed in.

"We are a nation in crisis, victimized by crime and conflict, frustrated by fear and failure," he began.

"A nation torn by war wants a restoration of peace.

Judy Agnew. (*Buffy Parker*)

"A nation plagued by disorder wants a renewal of order.

"A nation haunted by crime wants respect for law.

"A nation wrenched by division wants a rebirth of unity.

"If there is one great cry that rings clear, it is the cry for a leader.

"We have that man! . . .

"The final test of a man who seeks the Presidency is not what he promises but what he can do; not what he says but what he is.

"The man I nominate tonight is a President.

"When a nation is in crisis and when history speaks firmly to that nation that it needs a man to match the times—you don't create such a man; you don't discover such a man; you recognize such a man.

"It is my privilege to place in nomination for the office of President of the United States, the one man whom history has so clearly thrust forward—the one whom all America will recognize as a man whose time has come—the man for 1968, the Honorable Richard M. Nixon."

On August 9, 1968, the front-page headlines of the *New Yourk Times* read: NIXON SELECTS AGNEW AS HIS RUNNING MATE AND WINS APPROVAL AFTER FIGHT ON FLOOR: PLEDGES END OF WAR, TOUGHNESS ON CRIME.

When Judy Agnew left her hotel suite for her first press conference, she was still a bit shaky. "We heard about it ten minutes before the announcement came on television," she said. "My husband turned around and looked at me and said, 'I'm it.'"

Mrs. Agnew said that as soon as her husband got the news, by telephone, he shared it with her. "It was a surprise to both of us," she admitted. "We were both holding on to each other for a while, without saying a thing."

The fact that he was considered an "unknown" on the national political scene when Nixon chose him as a running

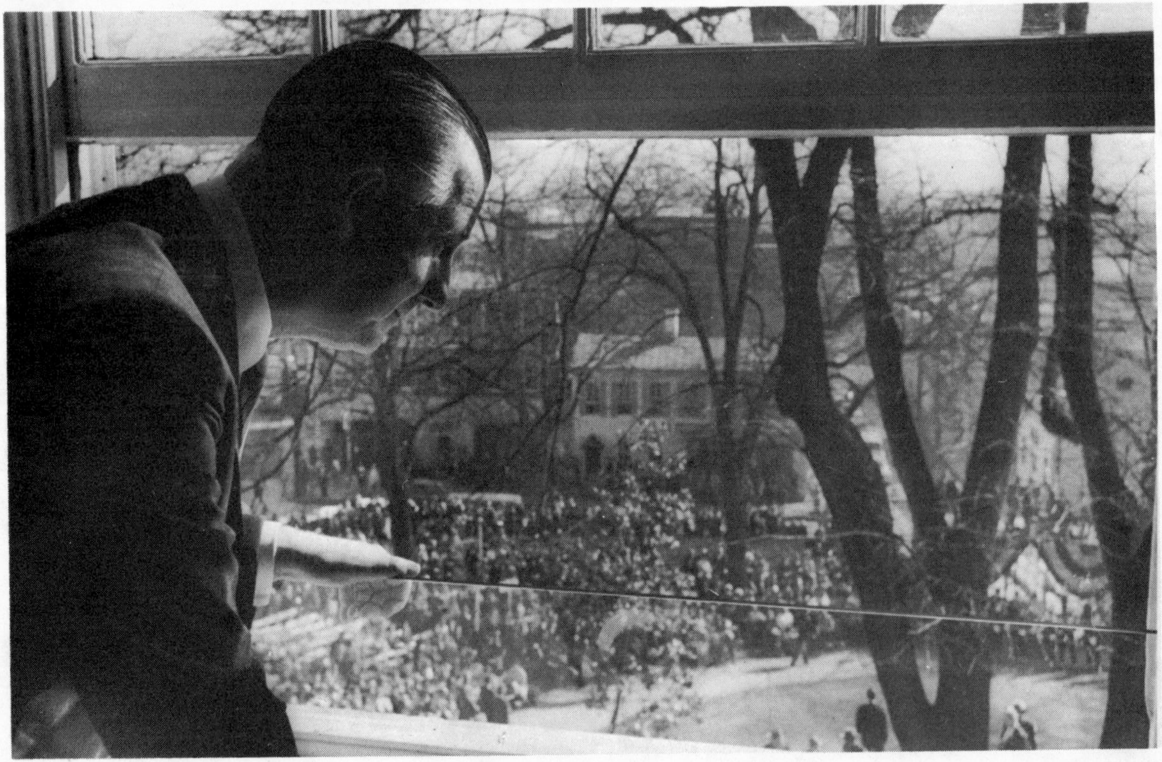

Wide World

mate does not disturb Governor Agnew. When he was advised by a reporter at his first press conference that the name Spiro Theodore Agnew was "not exactly a household word," the Governor smiled and predicted that it would be by November 5, 1968. Even tough reporters had to admit that Governor Agnew handled himself well, with candor, dignity, and good humor. In his own state the name Agnew has come to stand for a new kind of state government—one of vigor, imagination, and, above all, action. In a press conference, Richard M. Nixon said he was "completely confident" that Governor Agnew was fully qualified to take over as President.

Senator Tower of Texas was equally enthusiastic: "I believe that Ted Agnew is broadly representative of the mainstream of thinking in the party. He has a splendid record in championing civil rights and he believes this can be best achieved in an atmosphere of order."

Governor Agnew himself suggests with wry humor that he received neither exuberant hurrahs nor loud boos because he is a "fairly moderate person."

Yet in his first week of campaigning, he distinguished himself with decisive points of view. For example, he suggested that welfare payments should be uniform across the nation—no lower in Mississippi than in New York—to discourage the poor from crowding into the big cities. He said that the rural poor continue to migrate to already cramped cities because they get better welfare benefits. He suggested that welfare should be standardized nationally and perhaps administered by the Social Security program.

He believes in social justice within a framework of stability, and decries the oversimplification with which demagogues try to influence our society. "In the area of civil rights, as soon as you say you are for 'civil' anything, you are branded as being for the Negroes and if you are against 'civil' anything, you are against them. This is ridiculous. There is no soundness in those judgments."

The state of Maryland is known as America in miniature, a microcosm of our country. What Spiro Theodore Agnew has

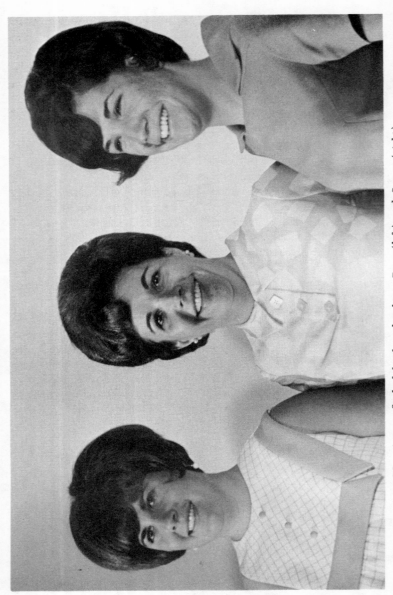

Mrs. Agnew flanked by her daughters Pam (left) and Susan (right). (*Wide World*)

achieved there, first as a responsible citizen, then as a forward-looking governor will be reflected in our country's future.

"This election is probably the most important in America's history," Agnew has said. "What is at stake is nothing less than survival, not of the Republican Party but of America as one nation, under God, indivisible, with liberty and justice for all."

At a meeting of the Portuguese-American Association in San Francisco, he said recently, "We must help the hungry and the poor, but let's stop overdramatizing what's wrong with the United States and start talking about what is right. I am tired of the criticism of the U.S. We are the most generous and compassionate people in the world."

That is the spur that will make Spiro T. Agnew a "household name" before November 5, 1968.

THE ISSUES AND WHERE HE STANDS

Today the footings of America are rotting while most of us stand fretfully by, watching with morbid curiosity.

The disease of our times is an artificial and masochistic sophistication—the vague uneasiness that our values are false, that there is something wrong with being patriotic, honest, moral or hardworking.

July 30, 1968

Some of my constituents in Maryland are contemplating an Agnew for Vice President campaign. This drive began almost immediately after we raised taxes, making it rather obvious that they are putting what they consider the best interests of their state before the best interests of their country.

Speech at the Republican Congressional Aides Luncheon
September 28, 1967

My claim to be a noncandidate of course parallels the assertions of Richard Nixon, George Romney, Nelson Rockefeller, Ronald Reagan, and Charles Percy. Therefore, I should probably announce that I am an eligible candidate for this great office so you will be convinced beyond a doubt that I am not.

Speech at the Republican Congressional Aides Luncheon
September 28, 1967

I share former Vice President Richard Nixon's view that the only thing worse than failing to fulfill a promise is making a promise fully cognizant that it cannot be fulfilled.

Testimony before the Republican
Task Force on Urban Affairs
Washington, D.C.
June 25, 1968

I doubt if any of us can imagine a Schlesinger or Galbraith pulling a Republican lever, but if their disenchantment is as sincere and desperate as their writings would indicate, they might well find themselves riding an elephant for lack of any other suitable transportation.

Speech at the Republican Congressional Aides Luncheon
September 28, 1967

I have little sympathy for the so-called hippie movement, because they would like to be the recipients of this mothering by the establishment so that their material wants will be satisfied and at the same time launch into attacks on the very system they depend on for survival.

Interview with the New York Times
August 25, 1968

On the United States' role as world policeman:

I don't think it's a question of being a policeman. I think it's a question of attempting to make certain that the free-

A campaign sign spells Agnew's name in Greek. (*Buffy Parker*)

enterprise system has a chance to move into actual nationally supported contention with communism. We've tried in our past foreign policy to sell Americanism instead of selling free enterprise.

Interview with the New York Times
August 25, 1968

On the role of the Vice-President:

The Vice-President must become convinced of the logic of the President's position. If it does such violence with his theory and philosophy, I guess he'd have nothing left to do but to resign if he was really seriously concerned about his disagreement with the President.

Interview with the New York Times
August 25, 1968

There is in this country a creeping paralysis of our national purpose, and we've got to do something about that. While there is hunger and poverty in this country, much of it is exaggerated. We must help the hungry and poor, but let's stop overdramatizing what's wrong with the United States and start talking about what is right. I'm tired of criticism of the United States. We are the most generous and compassionate people in the whole world.

Speech at the centennial dinner of the
Luso-American Fraternal Federation
San Francisco
August 12, 1968

The American people are not so naive as to believe the instant answer or the oversimplified solution. We live in a time too complex to require anything less than complicated solutions. We know more police patrolmen alone will not totally eliminate crime. We know that complete withdrawal from Vietnam will not secure lasting peace in Southeast Asia. We know that a negative income tax or a guaranteed annual wage is not the way to combat dependence but to perpetuate it.

Speech at the Rockville Republican Women's Club
Norbeck, Maryland
May 17, 1968

Senator Robert Kennedy's tragic death at the hands of a political assassin is an unmistakable sign that violence cannot be encouraged without reaping its horrible product. All those who are disciples of hate, who spew forth exhortations to burn and kill, must bear the responsibility for the deranged few who cross the line from talk to action.

Press statement
June 6, 1968

There are wars to be fought and battles to be won at home by citizens, as well as abroad by soldiers. . . . Each day the citizen must fight against abuse and apathy at home to give his victories as a soldier abroad real and vital meaning. We must fight a war against pollution of our air and water which menaces the physical health of our society at home as much as totalitarianism threatens the security of our democracy abroad.

We must fight against the frustrations of ignorance, prejudice, and poverty at home lest our cities become victims of perpetual violence and siege.

We must fight against the carnage on our highways which each year claims more lives than have been sacrificed by American soldiers in any single year of war—lives of noncombatants whose slaughter we have accepted with an appalling apathy.

Speech to the American Legion
Baltimore
July 19, 1967

44

Agnew shares a rostrum with Governor George Romney of Michigan.

(*Lee Troutner*)

At the highest levels of government, in the highest courts of our land, laws are being enacted and decisions are being rendered which, while not always popular, are pertinent to man's quest for dignity and man's effort to preserve that dignity. But where the quest has failed, where it has not reached, where it must finally turn to turn our times around, is in the area of individual human initiative and collective private action.

What practical progress can there be in the areas of employment, housing, education, and human renewal when our people resist command or indulge it stoically? How can we ever expect to remove blight, poverty, pollution, and ugliness from our lives when the government is willing but the citizen is not; when the State House is willing but the household is not; when the law is there but the spirit is not?

Speech at Lincoln Day Dinner
Youngstown, Ohio
March 4, 1967

The Vice-President must be aware of the fact that he must be prepared to assume the Presidency. This means that he must have a functioning, working knowledge of the foreign policy area. He can be ancillary to the President to a degree in operating in what you might call areas which aren't immediately crucial.

Interview with the New York Times
August 25, 1968

Now, as never before, America needs to remember our nation was forged by independence, character and just plain, individual guts. We've made so much rapid progress in terms of machines and possessions that we've forgotten that progress by people through principle is a slow and arduous affair. The success of big industry and big government seems to have left the American people materially rich and spiritually impov-

Governor and Mrs. Agnew at the inaugural ball, 1966. (*Wide World*)

erished. The heroic American is rapidly becoming the anxious American. The confidence of the American people that once could conquer a continent has been shaken to the core. We cower before the challenges we must face, we cringe where once we would tower.

Address to the Oklahoma Republican Party
Henryetta, Oklahoma
June 13, 1968

We need the federal government with its greater revenue resources to subsidize massive transportation projects, to develop "model cities," to administer a uniform welfare program. We do not, however, need excessive federal control or specific federal programs, for each community has its particular personality, its particular problems, and its particular priorities.

Speech before the Denver Metropolitan Symposium
December 4, 1967

In certain instances, we need and must have legislation and high-court action to enlarge human opportunities and protect human liberties. Of course we properly require the interest of government in the health of our communities and in the enrichment of our lives. *But we can do much by ourselves, by private effort;* sometimes with the help of government and many times without its slightest insistence or involvement.

The less we do, the more government is forced to do. The less we invest, the more tax dollars government must spend. This is a mathmatically unsound proposition and, in human terms, even more shameful. We can put a limitation on this waste by calling ourselves to action. We can do it better and we can do it cheaper.

Speech at Lincoln Day Dinner
Youngstown, Ohio
March 4, 1967

We seem to have lost all sense of proportion and perspective. Encouraged and abetted by the mass media, we have embarked upon a national whining catharsis.

We're so fascinated scrutinizing our exposed racism that we've forgotten the problems altogether.

July 30, 1968

We live in the best of times and the worst of times. Our problems are deep and desperate. Yet we have available greater resources and more knowledge than any people at any time in the history of the world.

Speech at Rockville Republican Women's Club
Norbeck, Maryland
May 17, 1968

The economic implications of neglect [in pollution control] are so tremendous and so terrifying that we can justify no less than a one hundred percent effort.

Address to Frederick (Maryland) Rotary Club
September 27, 1967

I think in some areas of pollution effort a business should be given an accelerated write-off of facilities it puts in—not to help it make its product better or produce more rapidly or in greater quantity, but simply to help the citizens around it live better lives through the lack of water pollution or air pollution.

Cumberland, Maryland
April 27, 1967

The right not to worship, alien though it may seem to us who believe in God, provides the only absolute guarantee that we will not later be told how and to what degree we must worship.

Address to Maryland State Constitutional Convention
Annapolis
September 29, 1967

"As one American citizen, it is my personal conviction that the security of America and the securing of Israel's rights and freedoms are one and inseparable, that in supporting the cause of Israel in its search for freedom and the right to live in peace, Americans are supporting the cause of the United States in its involvement with all the world's nations.

Speech to the Greater Washington
Jewish Community Foundation
Washington, D.C.
June 11, 1967

I think the kind of gun control law we need is a law that affects hand guns, guns that are readily concealable or rifles that break down to be readily concealable; a law that requires the person who wants to purchase them to obtain a permit with a sufficient waiting period so that the police can check to make certain that this person is not a psychopathic personality or a criminal or anyone who shouldn't be allowed to purchase a weapon. This type of control is reasonable.

Press conference
June 6, 1968

What is your duty as a citizen-soldier?

One: To conduct your personal life so that no aid or comfort is inadvertently given to the enemy. To assure that no nickel, dime, or dollar earned in your home is invested in the so-called innocent, illegal vices.

The table had to be raised with wooden blocks to accommodate the 6-foot, 2-inch Governor. (*Wide World*)

Two: To develop a reverence for law and a respect for those that enforce it within your home.

Three: To educate others by your example and deed, giving credence to your word.

Four: To commit yourself to be involved if it becomes necessary. . . . No one wants you to be a vigilante, no one drafts you to become an officer of the law . . . but you can and must report violations. You cannot abdicate or limit your civic responsibility to uphold the laws of our land.

Five: To develop police-community relations programs in your community if they do not exist. . . .

Six: To take the initiative in eliminating the environmental causes of crime in your community . . . slums, lack of recreational or employment opportunities. . . .

Seven: To demonstrate your confidence in your local law enforcement agency . . .

Eight: To encourage local officials to establish a Commission on Law Enforcement and the Administration of Justice which can study local problems in depth and provide immediate, community-oriented solutions.

Speech to the American Legion
Baltimore
July 19, 1967

In praise of free enterprise:

The Government never made a dollar.

Detroit
August 21, 1968

Administrative Philosophy

If a governor is to be fully and exclusively responsible to the people, the administrators of the executive branch must be fully and exclusively responsible to him.

Speech to Maryland State Constitutional Convention
Annapolis
September 29, 1967

One thing that has to be thoroughly recognized is that a governor of a minority party and working with a legislature cannot go around beating his breast and throwing his weight around.

Press conference
March 28, 1968

State government has a special role as the sovereign government closest to the people. It is immediate and intimate. It is the laboratory for political experiment, the instrument to test and apply new political solutions to new and old problems. State government, tempered by its unique constitutional safeguard of referendum, may yet become the most creative, imaginative, and dynamic form of political expression.

Speech to Maryland State Constitutional Convention
Annapolis
July 11, 1967

[In the first three months of my administration] we have changed from partisans locked in battle to partners joined in progress, from a government that was loathe to try to a government that refuses to fail. We have changed from a bland

53

Agnew just after his election as governor in 1966. (*Wide World*)

acceptance of the rising crime rate to an all-out attack upon it; from voicing a concern for education to the realization of a program to achieve it; from disregard for human rights to action which will help to break the barriers centuries have built. We have moved steadily from a fear of air and water pollution to some of the most progressive programs in the United States for its prevention and elimination; from an allegiance to archaic law to the pursuit of new directive; and in more than 750 separate acts of legislation put the past to rest and the future in perspective.

Speech to Rotary Ladies
Cumberland, Maryland
April 26, 1967

Maryland reflects the diversity that gave to America its greatness. We are many people. We are many races, religions, and national origins. We are a Tidewater people and a mountain·people. We are a people born to rich farmlands and a people reared in the teeming tempo of city streets. We are different kinds of people, each individual and unique, but united in our common love of freedom, our common respect for human liberty, our common passion for law and order, and our common faith in the future. A constitution for the State of Maryland is in every respect a constitution for each of the states united.

Speech to Maryland State Constitutional Convention
Annapolis
July 11, 1967

Today, the majority of America's elected governors are Republicans, and as governors we represent the only Republicans currently entrusted with high-level executive responsibility. The executive experience is singular in that it is the focal point which coordinates all administrative and legislative action required to implement policy. With all due respect,

I admit a Democrat—President Truman—best expressed the essence of executive responsibility when he said, "The buck stops here."

Speech to Rockville Republican Women's Club
Norbeck, Maryland
May 17, 1968

It cannot be overemphasized that for a constitution to endure it must be mainly limited to an expression of great principles.

What are these great universal principles? First, to secure and sustain the sovereignty of the people. Second, to protect and perpetuate the rights of the individual. Third, to create a political structure which safeguards the citizen by a series of checks and balances among . . . but not within . . . our three traditional branches. Fourth, to develop that superstructure for the state most conducive to efficient administration, effective legislation, and impartial adjudication. . . . Finally, to embrace a consistency of logic which reflects in the fewest words the fullest expression of a free society's solemn and voluntary contract with its government.

Speech to Maryland State Constitutional Convention
Annapolis
September 29, 1967

In referring to voting-age requirements, it is my intention to raise a question, not to criticize. I urge you to join me in serious consideration as to the logic and justice of retaining the traditional age of twenty-one years as a qualification for enfranchisement. If a man is old enough to die for his nation at eighteen, is he not old enough to vote? If a citizen is required to perform civic obligations—to pay taxes to and defend his government—is a responsible government not obligated to guarantee equivalent rights? . . . Is the attainment of twenty-one years of age a just, logical, pertinent, or valid qualification for enfranchisement?

Speech to Maryland State Constitutional Convention
Annapolis
September 29, 1967

People who are knowledgeable, who have no ax to grind in government, have agreed that this approach [a state income tax] of taxing income, of taxing ability to pay, is the way to approach the subject. We are not ashamed of our tax reform; we are proud of it. We don't go around the state hanging our heads about it like we are taking money out of the pockets of those who can least afford to pay it, because we know we are putting money in the pockets of those who can least afford to pay more.

Cumberland, Maryland
April 27, 1967

The Governor and General Assembly, who in the last analysis are responsible for raising funds to support all state programs, and who are held directly responsible by the electorate for any increase in the tax burden, must be permitted the right to exercise discretionary powers commensurate with this responsibility.

Speech to Maryland State Constitutional Convention
Annapolis
September 29, 1967

The uncontrolled wiretap and other snooping devices must be outlawed. Reasonable use of such surveillance is assured under the warrant procedures and court jurisdiction.

Speech to Maryland State Constitutional Convention
Annapolis
September 29, 1967

Our national Constitution has endured. For it was limited to an *expression of great principles;* founded upon the *faith* and *confidence* that the *righteousness* of these principles would suffice to provide security and direction for all future generations.

It is the most eloquently simple statement of principle ever inspired to direct a government and protect a people. Its relevance persevered through the recognition that, while institutions will change, great principles will endure.

The Constitution written for America one hundred and eighty years ago comes to us today unspoiled . . . yet the constitution written for Maryland eighty years later must now be edited anew. Like those immortal federalists who wrote the law of a nation, those who framed the constitutions for states were determined to rise above prejudice and write true to principle. But perhaps they rose too little and wrote too much.

Speech to Maryland State Constitutional Convention
Annapolis
July 11, 1967

Whichever concept, interpretation, or definition [of the Maryland constitution] you choose or reject, the worth of your work will be judged by history and tested by time.

You are the forefathers of the future, and while you may be privileged now to look ahead, you will not be privileged to look back once you have sealed the document and given it to the people for their approbation.

So look back *now* while you still may, for there is something to be learned and much to be remembered. Survey our national heritage for precedent that serves and tradition that inspires.

Speech to Maryland State Constitutional Convention
Annapolis
July 11, 1967

The inability of the old constitution to envisage growth and change is indicated by the 203 amendments which have been grafted to the original document. Even the fundamental construction was beset with flaws, not apparent when state government was small, but obstructive now that it has grown to impressive height. So distrustful were our predecessors of political authority that they created checks and balances *not only between* the three traditional branches of government *but within* them . . . not merely hindering administrative action but virtually strangling the implementation of bold solutions. . . .

The federal government, forced to fill the vacuum created by the strangled state, has grown out of all proportion to its constitutional purposes. In turn, the cherished constitutional balance between federal and state governments has been disrupted, and unless we act quickly and responsibly, it could be permanently destroyed.

Speech to Maryland State Constitutional Convention
Annapolis
July 11, 1967

Individual initiative and private enterprise, in most cases, can be more effective than government. In resolving the economic problems of the ghetto this means black capitalism, Negro ownership and management of commercial enterprises. . . .

Government's role should be limited to securing the opportunity for individual fulfillment. . . .

Government's role also extends to assuming that lawful avenues of redress are accessible to the citizens of the ghetto, to securing the pace and assuring the swift administration of justice.

July 30, 1968

Civil Rights

Constitutional safeguards must be devised not only to secure full and equal justice for all, but to guarantee that judicial treatment be swift in time, professional in performance, and consistent in quality.

Speech to Maryland State Constitutional Convention
Annapolis
September 29, 1967

As far as my civil rights position goes—it's going to be exactly consistent wherever I go. I think one of my biggest assets is that I try to be credible—and I want to be believed. That's one of the most priceless assets.

San Diego
August 13, 1968

Republican leadership will stand for civil rights but will not stand for civil disorders. I am proud—and I feel completely at home—in the company of men who espouse these principles.

As the first governer south of the Mason-Dixon line to secure passage of a state open housing law, to appoint Negroes to important state positions, and to recognize and implement the right of all to share in the responsibilities of government at the highest levels, I feel with Dick Nixon a deep concern for justice, not merely by the law, by the slogan, or by the promise, but by concrete and indisputable deed.

And as [one] who has condemned racism, deplored civil disorder, worked to separate good men from evil men, and resisted the pressure of the mob whether joined on the streets or on the campus, I share with Dick Nixon his concern for an

ordered society with justice for all where an excuse for breaking the law is only an excuse and never a justifiable one.

Keynote Address to Michigan Republican
State Convention
August 24, 1968

The central matter of our day is the very same as that of
Lincoln's time—only we express it not in terms of civil war
but civil rights, and not as a freeing of slaves but a realization
of equal civil opportunity. We are today as yesterday a house
divided, a nation torn, a people discomforted by doubt and
beset by fear. We are a hundred years past the Battle of
Gettysburg, but less than two years beyond the insurrection
at Watts. So much has changed, and so little.

Speech at Lincoln Day Dinner
Youngstown, Ohio
March 4, 1967

Somewhere the objectives of the civil rights movement
have been obscured in a surge of emotional oversimplification.
Somewhere the goal of equal opportunity has been replaced
by the goal of instantaneous economic equality. This country
does not guarantee that every man will be successful but only
that he will have an equal opportunity to achieve success. I
readily admit that this equal opportunity has not always been
present for Negroes—that it is still not totally present for
Negroes. But I say that we have come a long way. And I say
that the road we have trodden is built with the sweat of the
Roy Wilkinses and the Whitney Youngs—with the spiritual
leadership of Dr. Martin Luther King—and not with violence.

Tell me one constructive achievement that has flowed
from the madness of the twin priests of violence, Stokeley
Carmichael and Rap Brown. They do not build—they demolish.
They are agents of destruction and they will surely destroy us
if we do not repudiate them and their philosophies—along

Agnew at the graduation exercises of the European Division of the University of Maryland. To his left are West German Chancellor Kiesinger and Henry Cabot Lodge, U. S. Ambassador to Germany. (*Wide World*)

with white racists such as Joseph Carroll and Connie Lynch and the American Nazi Party, the John Birchers, and their fellow travelers.

Conference with civil rights and community leaders
Baltimore
April 11, 1968

Q. There's been a report [about] an amendment to the [Maryland] public accommodations bill that would permit tavern owners to refuse service to Negroes. Do you have any comment on that?

A. You know how I feel about public accommodations. I thought that any talk about going backwards in that area was a retreat into the Neanderthal age. I can't see any reason, under any circumstances, giving any consolation or hope to a retreat into the past in the area of public accommodations. The fears that were expressed in that area were proven to be absolutely without any foundation. All that reconsideration of these matters does is create hostility on the part of minority citizens, and I think it ought to be laid to rest.

Press conference
February 28, 1968

I have always been flatly opposed to artificial barriers of discrimination in places of public accommodation. A business whose prosperity is dependent upon the patronage of the general public has no right to deny any segment of the general public access to accommodation for arbitrary or discriminatory reasons.

Annapolis
June 27, 1967

It is not too late to return to the true target of the crusade for equality. That target is the elimination of all prejudice against Negroes in America and the provision of an equal opportunity to reach the top. That target will be realized when every man is judged on his own individual merit and only on his merit. Divisiveness and the doctrine of apartheid are impenetrable barriers between us and that target. With your help they can be torn down. . . . I publicly repudiate, condemn, and reject all white racists. I call upon you to publicly repudiate, condemn, and reject all black racists.

Conference with civil rights and community leaders
Baltimore
April 11, 1968

The biggest race questions that are arising today come, I submit to you, from the civil rights militants who are trying to create an unhealthy black racism in this country. And we've got to do something about that. I've always thought that the whole purpose of civil rights was one thing—that eventually, if everything goes the way we'd like it to go, I can sit down with a man of any color or creed and talk to him and not even think of the fact that he is a Negro or a white, or his religious affiliation, or anything about him. I can appraise him as an individual based on his individual work. That's what this is all about. Not black racism or white racism.

Press conference
June 20, 1968

The open housing bill has my fullest support. It now substantially conforms to the position I took well in advance of the 1966 [gubernatorial] election and which I have consistently held to since then—namely, to outlaw discrimination in the sale or rental of new housing, whether new homes or new apartments.

Annapolis
March 17, 1967

We, as employers in a free society, have always been generous and compassionate in hiring the worker handicapped by loss of sight or limb. Isn't it but a natural extension of our generosity and compassion to extend the hand of fellowship to the worker handicapped by the color of his skin, the blight of his surroundings, the poverty of his education and upbringing?

Speech at Lincoln Day Dinner
Youngstown, Ohio
March 4, 1967

I think a man can be totally pro-civil rights and totally against civil disobedience.

Seattle
August 19, 1968

Law and order must mean to all of our people the protection of the innocent—not to some the cracking of black skulls.
Speech to the 69th annual National Convention
of the Veterans of Foreign Wars
August 21, 1968

We have not provided an equal opportunity for all our citizens. In our frailty and human selfishness, we have too often shut our minds and our consciences to our black country-men. We need to respond to conscience rather than react to violence. We must aggressively move for progress—not out of fear of reprisal, but out of certain faith that it is right.

Detroit
August 21, 1968

Progress is not born of chaos nor compassion inspired by erosive force. Civil disorder is the mortal enemy of civil rights.
June, 1968

Last-minute check before the inauguration, 1966. (*Wide World*)

Health and Welfare

Well-motivated but poorly coordinated attempts to solve the perplexing health problems of our society are failing. Let us frankly admit that all levels of government and the myriad specialized groups of the private health sector are responsible to varying degrees for the crisis that is imminent [and] act quickly to avert it.

Annapolis
January 22, 1968

Recently, the courts have ruled that chronic alcoholics cannot be imprisoned for public inebriation. If many of our streets are not to become skid rows, we must provide facilities other than jails for alcoholics.

Press statement
January 4, 1968

A comprehensive program [on alcoholism] will be developed, and the aid of industry, labor, and other sectors of the general public will be enlisted for an overall campaign.

It is time we recognize alcoholism for what it is—a sickness that saps and debilitates our society, and not a crime that can be controlled by filling jails with persons arrested for public drunkenness.

Annapolis
August 31, 1967

Q. Do you think there is a possibility that the state [Maryland] might sometime take over the publicly operated hospitals such as city hospitals and others in the counties?

67

A. I sincerely hope it will never be necessary for the state to actually get into the hospital business. I can see a potential if we cannot solve these problems through this course that someday a state agency—a regulatory agency of the nature of the Public Service Commission—may have to come into being to regulate the hospital area. But I am hopeful that the private sector interested in health, given this opportunity, will be able to solve the problem without governmental intervention.

Press conference
Annapolis
January 22, 1968

I have always felt that the question of abortions is properly a medical question, not a legal question. I understand the concern of certain religious groups over abuses of the situation and I understand the contentions as to the rights of the unborn. I agree that certainly unborn citizens do have rights, but I think we have to understand one thing—that the physician when he is faced with a medical decision for which he is qualified and for which he is trained, he should be able to make the judgment. Certainly none of us likes to see the life of a mother jeopardized or the future life of the child jeopardized when it becomes apparent on sound medical reasoning to the physician that this child cannot lead a normal happy life and, in effect, may be jeopardizing not only his own future but the future of his own parents—of the mother—by going through the birth. This is not an easy question but, as medical science progresses, my inclination is to go along with the doctors and let them make the decision.

Press conference
January 9, 1968

Day care for the elderly is an exciting innovation in geriatric services, with a potentially important contribution to

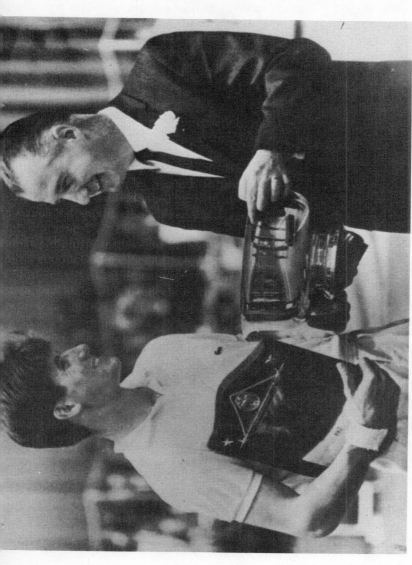

Agnew presents a silver bowl to Charles Pasarell, who has just won the U. S. Indoor Tennis Championship. (*Wide World*)

make in saving both financial and human resources . . . Most significantly [day care centers] provide essential services for those who might be prematurely institutionalized due to the inability of their family or friends to meet their special needs on a full-time basis.

Such facilities can help conquer and postpone mental deterioration—which is often considered a normal aspect of the aging process but which can also be attributed to such factors as alienation or isolation from the community, the tensions involved when a family must provide constant care for an aged relative, malnutrition due to inability to shop and prepare foods, or minor physical ailments.

News release
Towson, Maryland
October 26, 1966

An immediate criticism to national standardized welfare payments arises from the varying costs of living in different sections of the country. Admittedly, a dollar buys more in Arkansas than in New York. But standardized social security payments are universally accepted, and standardized welfare payments are no less logical. Second, standardization could serve as a positive force, making it not only possible but profitable to remain in a rural, underdeveloped area. Once the uneducated, unemployed population is stabilized—at federal expense—states and cities could afford to initiate meaningful programs at the local level related to local employment opportunities and manpower needs. How can you solve the job problem, when the unemployed won't stay put?

A national welfare program provides a healthy, economical alternative to present and proposed policies. Tremendous duplication already exists as a result of the federal, state, and local governments all being in the welfare business. The current federal effort alone is a bewildering kettle of

A gathering of governors on the convention floor in Miami—Romney, Agnew, Shafer, Rhodes and Kirk. (*Wide World*)

alphabet soup involving HEW, OEO, HUD, and a cast of thousands.

Testimony before the Republican Task Force
on Urban Affairs
Washington, D.C.
July 25, 1968

Welfare benefits have to be standardized if we're ever going to stop the flow of the urban poor into the impacted areas. I feel very strongly that the welfare program should be nationally administered. I think it would be a very economical way to do it.

Interview with the New York Times
August 25, 1968

Education

Ultimately, education is the tool to break the vicious cycle of poverty, prejudice, and public dependence. We cannot negate or neglect the truth that compensatory education is an imperative for the deprived child. Only a better than average education can propel the child with a worse than average background into the American mainstream.

Speech before the Denver Metropolitan Symposium
December 4, 1967

From the day he enters first grade, the disadvantaged or neglected child faces handicaps unlike his more affluent contemporaries. Without the early assistance which day care can help promote, his lack of verbal skills and proper orientation for the educational experience often means that he steadily drops behind in school . . . to become the drop-out . . . to

enjoy limited expectations at best, or become a burden on society at worst.

How much misery could be avoided, how much saving of state dollars, by reaching the child early enough to lessen the chance of later delinquency?

Press statement
Towson, Maryland
October 26, 1966

We cannot afford to temporize or be timid, to postpone or procrastinate. Education is our surest instrument to guarantee individual fulfillment. Education is our ultimate instrument to assure social and economic progress. Education is the only inheritance we can bestow upon our children that no adversity, excepting death itself, can destroy. Our future as individuals, as a state, and as a nation is totally dependent upon our educational system. Our progress as a people will be no swifter than our progress in education, for the human mind is our fundamental resource.

Speech to the Maryland Congress of Parents and Teachers
Baltimore
November 3, 1967

Attitude training should be instituted within our schools as a co-equal partner of academic education. By accommodating the immediate and significant environmental and social problems of our day within our public school curricula, we can increase the awareness and ability of our next generation to respond to the challenges of the future; to reject all that is wrong and to respect and revitalize all that is right within our society. Prejudice and pollution, crime and delinquency, narcotics and sex should be approached frankly, honestly, and promptly by our public schools.

Speech before the Denver Metropolitan Symposium
December 4, 1967

John Lubbock, Lord Avebury, wrote: "The important thing is not so much that every child should be taught, as that every child should be given the wish to learn." Today as never before this principle must guide our educational policies and programs.

We live in history's most exciting, challenging, and formidable moment—the era of the knowledge explosion. In the last twenty-five years, mankind has acquired more scientific information than in all previous history. Ninety percent of all the scientists that ever lived are alive and working today. Emerging evidence indicates that seventy percent of all knowledge destined to support our present students during their lifetime is as yet unknown and undiscovered; that a student expecting to earn his livelihood with his hands will have to learn new techniques at least *six* times before his retirement.

Thus we cannot hope to provide our students with sustaining skills, secure technical truths, constant or comprehensive knowledge. But we can provide them with the attitude to adapt; the confidence and courage to accept rapid change; the ability to continuously learn; the emotional security to regard change as an exciting challenge.

The first responsibility rests with the parents. Comprehension and confidence, an attitude to accept change, and an appetite to constantly learn can best begin in the cradle, not the kindergarten. We must prepare our children to cope with the pressures and anxieties that have become commonplace.

Speech to the Maryland Congress of Parents and Teachers
Baltimore
November 3, 1697

The Republican Party

Some people called the Republican convention in Miami dull. After all, we didn't have a thousand delegates whose credentials were challenged. We didn't have a floor fight, or the threat of one, over policy on Vietnam. We didn't have a march on the convention by the hippies or yippies. We simply conducted an open and businesslike convention where every candidate was heard, where a great platform was written, and where the next President of the United States was given a mandate to take his message to America. . . .

And when we win, we're just liable to bring back into American life a lot of things that the devotees of the so-called "new politics" consider dull. Dull things like patriotism. Dull things like incentive. Dull things like a respect for law and a concern for a greater justice for all Americans. In fact, things could become so dull that some little old ladies who wear sneakers to get a fast start on criminals on city streets might go back to wearing high heels. And some of the fellows hanging around the street corner might want to go to work again just to block out the boredom from their lives.

After years and years of living by electric shock, a cool summer and a safe street might take some getting used to. It might be unspectacular to some to have an administration in Washington that maintained the value of the dollar and kept prices steady, that put an end to the gold drain, that stopped the pirating of American ships on the high seas, and that discontinued American casualties in Southeast Asia. All this might be boring to some, but what a welcome change it would be to most Americans.

Keynote Address to the Michigan
Republican State Convention
August 24, 1968

This campaign is based on a desire, I think, of the American people for moderation.

Baltimore
August 14, 1968

At this critical juncture in America's history, the Republican Party stands as a resolute and responsible alternative to *all* who vote their conscience and their principles.

76

The Republican Party, born in an era of civil crisis and civil war, is prepared to face the truth, the present and the future. We're a party linking a broad spectrum of political views, because we're the party *of* and *for* the individual. Yet, for all our diversity in particulars, no party is more firmly united in principles. We love our nation and stand proud of our unabashed patriotism. We are the party born in the determination to preserve country and Constitution. We remain steadfast in this commitment.

We appreciate, with an intensity impossible to articulate, the greatness of America's democratic system. We are frankly reverent of the wisdom of our nation's Constitution and frankly appalled by those who would destroy the fabric that binds our nation.

We hold fast to the law in the faith that only with law is progress possible.

We are the party that regards individual rights as inseparable from individual responsibilities. We have great hopes for collective and individual fulfillment, and we expect each individual to contribute to his own and society's progress. We believe in independence, not license. We believe in opportunity, not anarchy. We believe in compassion, not concession. This is not conservatism, nor is it liberalism. It is Americanism. I want to preserve our nation and I believe the overwhelming majority of 200 million Americans stand with me.

And if anyone or any force within this nation or this planet thinks the American people are going to surrender in the face of continuous crises, they are wrong. The American people may be temporarily confused, but the American people will not collapse. We shall survive the threat of Communism abroad and chaos at home. We shall emerge a stronger and more perfect nation.

Speech to Maryland Republican State Convention
Annapolis
June 22, 1968

Republican Headquarters

We must now set about selling the case for Republicanism, and with it a new image, to the American public. But first we must do some unselling. We must lay to permanent rest the notion that our party is partner to special privilege, wealth, and parochialism. We must unsell the idea that we are more concerned with the public ledgers than we are with the public good. We must correct the impression that we regard big government as at all times bad, or massive spending as in every instance evil. We must refuse to tolerate the role of a minority party, the yesterday party, the protest party, the white Anglo-Saxon party, the rural America party, the stand-pat party.

Once we are cleansed of undeserving images we may set about purifying American society. And the very first thing we must do is to make a sacred covenant with the people that we will tell the truth, the whole truth, and at all times the truth. Never before in our history has leadership had its credibility so seriously questioned or its integrity so nakedly challenged.

Speech to Yale University Young Republicans
April 19, 1967

Great nations collapse only when their foundations decay. Today, the footings of America are rotting while most of us stand fretfully by, watching with morbid curiosity. The disease of our times is an artificial and masochistic sophistication—a vague uneasiness that our values are corny—that there is something wrong with being patriotic, honest, moral, or hard-working. The sneer of the nonconformist has become an effective weapon for those who cannot achieve within the framework of our society and, therefore, seek to destroy it.

Above all, as Republicans we should adhere to our proven values. I believe we agree that guaranteed employment is preferable to guaranteed income. Private investment is preferable to public spending. Local initiative is more effective than federal infringement. If America is to have revolution let it be

79

one of ideas and approaches; let it occur in Congress rather than the streets. We cannot stand still for lawlessness and, with progressive laws, we will not stand still.

Testimony before the Republican Task Force on Urban Affairs
Washington, D.C.
June 25, 1968

The present Democratic Party leadership has lost the nation's confidence but this does not imply the Republican Party will automatically win it. We must work for it and we will need every hand available.

Speech at Rockville Republican
Women's Club
Norbeck, Maryland
May 17, 1968

The American people are suffering from government so interested in achieving ends that it uses and excuses any means. We have reaped the hideous product of a society so permissive it has pointed our nation toward the brink of anarchy. Campus rebellions are symptoms of this permissiveness run rampant— where students demand and faculties capitulate. Even more terrifying and tragic are the assassinations of national leaders— this is the legacy of lenience with the lawless.

Speech to the Oklahoma Republican Party
Henryetta, Oklahoma
June 13, 1968

We must put an end to government by expedience, to the theory that public favor can be bought by massive social spending. We must put an end to practices which stifle private enterprise and suffocate individual initiative. We must provide each citizen every opportunity to fulfill his aspirations. We must restore law and order, and work through law to achieve a new

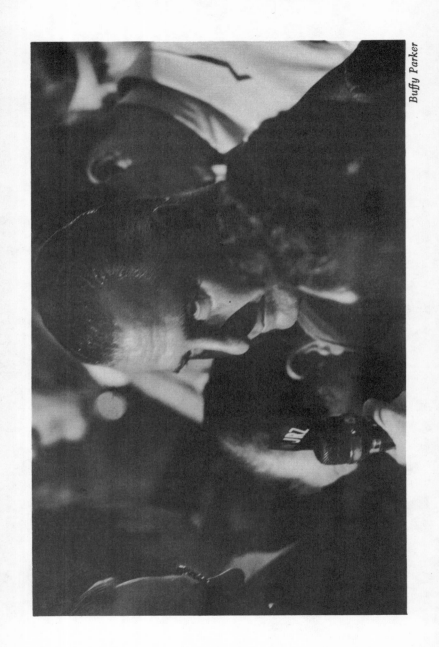

and more perfect order. We must combat prejudice because it is ignorant and evil and wasteful. We must eliminate poverty by eliminating dependence, not perpetuating it. We must have peace at home and abroad. The way may not be easy nor the answers instant, but all this can be done. We are the most advanced and affluent nation in the world. We cannot be defeated by force from without—only by conflict and confusion within our country.

Speech to Maryland Republican State Convention
Annapolis
June 22, 1968

The Republican Party offers the American people a return to government by principle. Government by expedience—the instant answer and the easy way out—has failed.

Speech to New Jersey Federation of Republican Women
Atlantic City
May 9, 1968

We must become realistic if we are to elect a Republican to the most important post of power in the world. We must become open-minded and tough-minded . . . We must face the truth that Republicans have been wrong more times than right in their choice of campaigns, communications, and candidates. This is why there are more bull asses than bull elephants in Washington today.

Luncheon Speech at the Congressional Aides
September 28, 1967

The country is in crisis. We face a foreign crisis, a domestic crisis and a moral crisis. That's what the 1968 election will be all about. And that's why the Republican Party confronts great obligations as well as great opportunities. . . .

We must have peace at home and peace abroad. Permanent peace can come only through strength. Too often our

nation has lost the war at the conference table, not on the battlefield. The Republican Party cannot claim a monopoly as the Peace Party. Yet the twentieth-century presidents from Theodore Roosevelt to Dwight D. Eisenhower are famous for getting America *out of* and not into wars, and keeping the peace throughout the world. The Republican Party offers the American people a fresh path to peace through principle, not compromise forged from past failures. . . .

The Republican Party offers the American people a choice —the choice of strong, honest leadership. And when I speak of "strong" leadership, I do not mean strong in the popularity polls but strong on principle. When I speak of "honest" leadership, I speak of a leader who has the courage to tell the public the truth. Now, as never before, there is a great need for America's leaders to talk forthrightly and frankly, to emphasize realism and not rhetoric.

Speech to New Jersey Federation of Republican Women
Atlantic City
May 9, 1968

Principle is the key to the Republican thrust. Principle is the alternative to the Democratic Party's philosophic answer to all problems—expedience! We have seen where government by expedience has brought us. We are tired of a damn-the-details, full-speed-ahead attitude. . . .

Speech at Rockville Republican
Women's Club
Norbeck, Maryland
May 17, 1968

Our stake in this campaign is nothing less than national survival . . . not of the Republican Party . . . but of America as "one nation, under God, indivisible, with liberty and justice for all." To this great national purpose, let us rededicate ourselves. Then we shall enjoy not only the euphoria that comes with winning but also the deeper satisfaction that comes with knowing we deserve to win.

*Keynote Address to the Michigan
Republican State Convention
August 24, 1968*

Urban Problems

An unholy alliance between big cities and the federal government has developed which could devastate the principle and purpose of our federal system. There is a measure of historical justification for this situation since state governments—prior to reapportionment—often failed to take interest in, or responsibility for, urban problems. However, this neglect has been largely corrected. Today, state governments are well prepared and eager to participate in urban programs. We realize that the problem of America is the problem of the cities—that one percent of American land where 70 percent of Americans live. We recognize that almost every state's prosperity is ultimately linked to its one or several commercial centers. If these are allowed to decay or implode, the wealth of the entire state can erode and eventually disappear.

*Testimony before the Republican Task Force on Urban Affairs
Washington, D.C.
June 25, 1968*

The President claims to have provided $30 billion in federal aid to the cities. Yet in testimony before a Senate subcommittee, his Budget Director, Charles Schultze, set the figure at $10.3 billion . . . and even this lesser figure includes $2.1 billion for the construction of urban expressways, which hardly help the poor whose homes lie in interstate highways' paths.

*Speech before the Denver Metropolitan Symposium
December 4, 1967*

Taxation may be used creatively at the local level to encourage optimum land use or coercively to discourage the exploitation of blight. At the present time our urban assessment policies sometimes promote speculation in slum properties by absentee landlords who realize returns out of all proportion to investment and assessed valuation. If substandard housing was assessed with a view to its potential optimum rather than present value, the perpetuation of this type of abuse would be readily checked. A permissive attitude in this area means the total community is not only condoning exploitation but actually subsidizing the exploiter.

Speech before the Denver Metropolitan Symposium
December 4, 1967

State governments are well prepared and eager to participate in urban programs [for] almost every state's prosperity is ultimately linked to its one or several commercial centers. If these are allowed to decay or explode, the wealth of the entire state can erode and disappear.

Nor are we so naïve as to believe there is any one urban panacea—any more than there is any *one* urban problem. The problems of the city are as profuse as they are profound— blight, pollution, and traffic snarls compete with poverty, prejudice, and ignorance. If we are even to begin to attempt solutions, we must focus all the resources and talent of both the public and private sectors of our economy upon the problems. The job cannot be done by federal-city alliances, nor even by the federal, state, and local governments cooperatively. It can be done only by all levels of government working in concert with business and industry, supported by all types of citizens. It can be done only by enlisting the imagination of the private sector and instituting daring new ideas and programs.

Speech to Maryland Manufacturers Association
Baltimore
November 17, 1967

Urban renewal inevitably displaces more people than it can accommodate, and unless the dislocated and displaced are accommodated the project simply stimulates the transfer of blight and impaction to another vulnerable area.

Speech before the Denver Metropolitan Symposium
December 4, 1967

We not only care, we offer a realistic and immediate answer to the despair of the ghetto. We propose to build initiative, not to perpetuate dependence. Our solution is not black power but green power—the power of the purse—Negro enterprise and industry. Our way is not to separate America into two societies, black and white, but to see that all of society shares the benefits our nation has to offer.

Keynote Address to the Michigan
Republican State Convention
August 24, 1968

If progress is to come in the next decade, we must begin with the young. The problems [of the ghetto] are awesome; the need for fresh vision and dialogue is imperative. Here we have to overcome not only the barriers of racial misunderstanding and economic deprivation but the very real gulf between generations.

Memorandum sent to Human Relations Committee
staff member
April 25, 1968

Needless to say, I am looking for the student leader, the excellent student, even graduate students, or successful young men and women in the community. While I am not opposed to including militants within the law, I obviously cannot work with those who would counsel or condone operating outside

Lee Troutner

the law. This I do not mean in any narrow sense; it includes those who would advocate burning draft cards as well as cities.

*From Governor Agnew's proposal
to form a Governor's Youth
Council of Negro college
students to advise him on
ghetto problems
April 25, 1968*

You've got to change the environment; this is the key that is being neglected in this situation. You can put all the money you want into a program that's supposed to improve the ghetto areas of a big city, and if you leave the impaction, it's a self-infecting situation, the change is temporary and the compression of the people against each other and the futile effect of any individual attempting to raise himself to a level above that of his neighbors is self-evident.

*Interview with the New York Times
August 25, 1968*

Vietnam

I am convinced that the reason we are debating the war in Vietnam so openly and antagonistically is because it was not faithfully described at its outset. It is suspicion and not a lack of patriotism that makes the hawk impatient, the dove resentful.

*Speech to Yale University Young Republicans
April 19, 1967*

Some people in our free society want to believe that freedom can be defended without sacrifice, without the loss of life

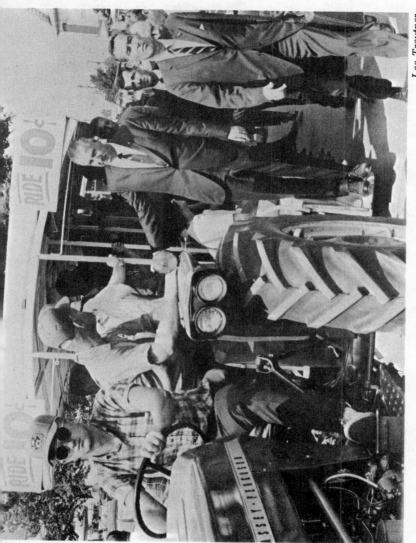

and the firing of guns. These are people too young to know of the great wars or too prone to forget the reasons for which they were fought.

Some people in our free society believe we can escape the cruel reality of power conflict by picking flowers and writing poems, by growing beards and singing songs. These are people who say war at any price is bad and peace at any cost is good.

Some people in our free society think it will all just go away once we stop thrusting our ideas on other nations and begin to practice at home the freedom we preach abroad. These people are well-meaning and sensitive Americans but forget that what has driven men to evil before has not yet been totally conquered and might never be. . . .

When nations fail, nations fight. When words fail, guns fire. The bullet inevitably carries the message that somebody else would not or could not deliver. . . .

While we have not became so cynical as to believe war is an inevitable and irrefutable product of the human condition, neither can we delude ourselves that the forces of tyranny and evil will retreat without continuous opposition.

Speech to the American Legion
Baltimore
July 19, 1967

I don't feel that we can unilaterally stop the bombing in Vietnam. I think the President's position that this can't simply be a unilateral situation is very realistic but they must give us some assurances that they will take steps to de-escalate hostilities concurrently.

Interview with the New York Times
August 25, 1968

I have a son in Vietnam near Hue, right now. I want him home very much—I'm worried to death about him. But I don't see how pulling out without really meeting the problem of

ending this thing is going to do other than cause us to fight
the war again.

Interview with the New York Times
August 25, 1968

Civil Disorders

Free democracy is built upon a single great promise—
civil rights must be balanced by civil responsibilities. Rapidly,
this principle has been corroded. Civil disobedience has inevitably led to civil disorder.

Speech at Rockville Republican Women's Club
Norbeck, Maryland
May 17, 1968

Civil disobedience, at best, is a dangerous policy, since
it opens the path for each man to be judge and jury of which
laws are unjust and may be broken. Moreover, civil disobedience leads inevitably to riots, and riots condoned lead inevitably to revolution—which, incidentally, is a word we are
hearing more and more frequently from advocates of black
power.

Capitulation to violence, either to keep the peace or from
misguided compassion, is suicidal for society.

While hardening of attitudes and polarization is paralyz-
ing, an acceptance of mass guilt coupled with an abrogation
of individual responsibility could be disastrous for this great
country of ours.

July 30, 1968

If one wants to pinpoint the cause of riots, it would be
this permissive climate and the misguided compassion of pub-

lic opinion. It is not the centuries of racism and deprivation that have built an explosive crescendo but the fact that law-breaking has become a socially acceptable and occasionally stylish form of dissent.

July 30, 1968

What is the freedom that you as soldiers fought for abroad worth if you are afraid to walk alone at night at home? What value can be placed upon your contribution as a citizen to our national prosperity if your person and property are menaced? . . . We must fight for domestic security on our streets with the same intensity and passion that we have brought to the defense of our national security.

Address to the American Legion
Baltimore
July 19, 1967

You cannot see your cities burned beneath your eyes and not expect to question deeply and, perhaps, to change. . . . If peace and progress are to replace tension and turbulence in America's cities, law and order must first be restored.

Speech at Rockville Republican Women's Club
Norbeck, Maryland
May 17, 1968

Racial discrimination must be eliminated no matter whom that upsets. . . . But anarchy and rioting have no constructive purpose in a constitutional republic.

Acceptance speech
Republican National Convention
August 8, 1968

It is time that public offiicals in this country stopped yield-ing to pressures and threats and intimidations by those who

Wilt Chamberlain towers above Agnew and Nixon as "The Stilt" joins them to discuss campaign activities. (*Wide World*)

would take the law in their own hands. I certainly don't intend to yield to such pressures.

Press statement
March 30, 1968

This willingness to tolerate individual irresponsibility under any circumstances other than insanity can crumble the walls of a constitutional democracy. For democracy is sustained through one great premise: that civil rights are balanced by civil responsibilities. My right to life, liberty, and the pursuit of happiness is secure only so long as I respect your right to life, liberty, and the pursuit of happiness. I can claim no right as a human or as a citizen that you cannot claim under the law.

In excusing individual responsibility we condone lawlessness and encourage cynical leaders to exploit the madness of the mob. We tacitly endorse such inflammatory statements as Rap Brown's "violence is as American as cherry pie." Remarks like this, widely and cheerfully disseminated by the media, have created a belief that rioting is the inalienable right of the ghetto resident.

If one wants to pinpoint the cause of riots, it would be this permissive climate and the misguided compassion of public opinion. It is not the centuries of racism and deprivation that have built to an explosive crescendo but the fact that law-breaking has become a socially acceptable and occasionally stylish form of dissent. . . . If we reward violence, violence will soon supplant law as the accepted instrument to achieve social change. Yet if we deny that just grievances exist, we destroy society just as surely by blocking effective outlets for change. Prevention, not repression, must be our end and the law, not counterforce, must be our means.

Address to Seventeenth International Conference
of the Greek Orthodox Youth of America
New York City
July 30, 1968

Buffy Parker

The riots in our cities [are] caused in all too many cases not just by evil conditions but by evil conditions and evil men. We must confront the evil conditions and the evil men that exploit them. Too often and too long our nation's intellectual, spiritual, and political leaders have countenanced, condoned, and even counciled with such men. If our nation is not to move toward two societies—separate and unequal, white and black—America must condemn those extremists, whether white or black, who prey upon racism.

Speech at Rockville Republican Women's Club
Norbeck, Maryland
May 17, 1968

It is evident that there is ample cause for unrest in our cities. There is still discrimination and, in too many cases, there are deplorable slum conditions. Our Negro citizens . . . are not receiving equal educational, job, and housing opportunities. The gains recently made, while good, are not enough.

I believe that responsible militants within the Negro leadership should use every means available to place legitimate pressure on those in authority to break the senselss and artificial barriers of racial discrimination. But legitimate pressure —the power of the vote, the power of organized political, economic, and social action—does not give any person or group license to commit crimes.

Burning, looting, and sniping, even under the banner of civil rights, are still arson, larceny, and murder. There are established penalties for such felonies, and we cannot change the punishment simply because the crime occurred during a riot. The laws must be consistently enforced to protect all our people. If an angry man burns his neighbor's house, or loots his neighbor's store, or guns his neighbor down, no reason for his anger will be enough of an excuse.

July 30, 1967

To all who have been victimized, I pledge to you that all possible power will be exerted to restore order and security to your lives, and to assist those made homeless by fire.

To those few who loot and burn we shall show no sympathy, nor will we tolerate those few who could take the law into their own hands. We have local police, state police, and federalized troops on the scene, in control, working effectively. We ask for no citizen volunteers, only common sense from our citizens.

While today we are pressed to confront force with force, to put down violence and douse fires, the lessons of these past hours have not been lost on any of us.

We know now as never before how vital is the law to our liberty.

We know now as never before that violence is no friend of freedom, and that the mob is no ally of civil rights.

We know now as we've always known that where rightful grievances exist, we must redress them with speed and compassion.

We know now that to move ahead we must never stand still. We must not stand still for a violation of our laws. Nor must we stand still for conditions which create hopelessness or despair.

We must press on, at once, for the good jobs, the good housing, the good education, for all those of our citizens who have been long denied these opportunities.

Let us rededicate ourselves to the unfinished business, not out of fear of reprisal but out of certain faith that it is right.

> *Address to the citizens of Maryland after declaring a state of emergency in Baltimore*
> *April 7, 1968*

Q. Do you concur, Governor, in the basic finding of the Kerner Commission that the cause of the riots last summer was the white racist attitude of our society?

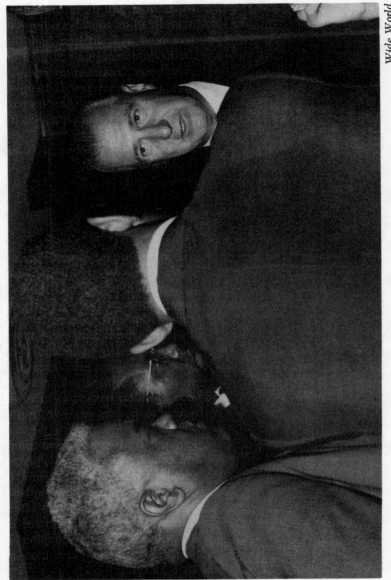

A.   Well I don't think it's that simple. I think that this is a contributing cause. I think that black racism is another contributing cause. I wouldn't want to be placed in a position where I had to apportion the fault, because that's impossible. But . . . I think it is important to remember that racism of either type is very harmful to our progress and very harmful to the accord that we need to get the job done.

Q.   Governor, the Kerner Commission report says that it is of the "utmost importance" for governors and mayors to keep open lines of communication with Negro leaders, including specifically young militants. Do you take exception to that?

A.   Well, I think militants fall into two categories. I have never found an accurate definition of the word "militant." If by militant you are simply being outspoken and aggressive and striving for what you think is necessary to effect reforms which you believe in, I have no objection to it. If by being militant you are talking about setting fires and looting stores, then I want no part, regardless of the Kerner Commission or not, in communicating with that type of militant. Now let me say this, the mere fact that someone may have espoused unlawful activity and been a militant recognized in that sense does not forever preclude him from coming into communication with this administration. If these people will recognize that the way to orderly change is through the law and will frankly come and ask for meetings with me in recognition and in dedication of using lawful means, I would not let the fact that they have previously stepped over the line interfere with my communicating with them.

Press conference
April 18, 1968

As Governor of this state, I cannot and will not tolerate riot-induced felonies which verge on anarchy, nor will I allow the individuals who maliciously inspire such action to slip away unchallenged. Such people cannot be permitted to enter

a state with the intention to destroy and then sneak away leaving these poor people with the results of their evil scheme.

Press statement
July 25, 1967

Q. Governor, do you feel there is any merit in Mayor Daley's order to the Chicago police to shoot arsonists and looters?

A. I think it's an oversimplified reaction and an oversimplified approach. No one can make a judgment on what to do in a situation like that unless he is a professional who is on the scene in full cognizance of the surrounding situations. Now I would say, to use a couple of extreme examples: to shoot a twelve-year-old child who is seen with a box of matches stooping near a building would be the height of callousness; I'd say on the other hand if a man had hurled a Molotov cocktail into a pile of gasoline-soaked rags in a building that was going up in flames and there were people sleeping in that building, I wouldn't hesitate for a minute if I were a law enforcement officer to shoot him if he didn't stop on my command to stop. You can't just generalize this. The surrounding circumstances are the things that must govern.

Q. The main controversy concerns looters rather than arsonists.

A. Well, I think it would have to be a pretty extreme situation, and I doubt if I could visualize a situation offhand tht would justify shooting down someone who is taking a commodity out of a store. I think it's like killing an ant with an ax.

Press conference
April 18, 1968

I don't approve of blanket endorsement of shooting [at rioters] under any circumstances. We have some much more sophisticated methods of dealing with looters today than we

had when simply firing a weapon was the answer. We have
this deterrent gas that has been used most effectively in riots,
and I think it's a matter of an individual and professional
police judgment as to what lengths force will be resorted to.
. . . The evaluation has to be made at the scene of the riot
and under the conditions that are present, by a professional
person.

Annapolis
January 3, 1968

Crime

If we are to successfully combat crime, [we must make]
a larger effort to rehabilitate the environment which breeds
and sustains crime. The struggle against poverty, slums,
ignorance, and prejudice is overwhelming in scope and by its
very nature slow and gradual. But unless we prevail in this
effort, all others will be for naught. It encompasses the whole
spectrum of our community life—education, family organiza-
tion, employment opportunities, and housing. . . . I think we
should take a more realistic approach to our attack on crime.
I believe that too much emphasis has been placed on the
"innovative functions" and not enough on the practical day-
to-day problems of our law enforcement and correctional
officers. . . . I cannot help but feel that we are overlooking
the "nuts and bolts" of this problem. We should be putting
more and better qualified law enforcement officers on the
street, more and better qualified correctional officers in our
penal institutions, and finally, more and better qualified
officers in a position to supervise our parole and probation
subjects.

Statement to the House Judiciary Committee
May 9, 1967

Unlike foreign wars, the state and local governments will direct the course of battle in [the] domestic war on crime. The federal government will provide support and suggest direction, but primary responsibility for community tranquility remains vested in the state government. Therefore, the relative success of combat will depend on the ability of state leadership and the intensity of community support.

Address to the American Legion
Baltimore
July 19, 1967

Q. Governor, what's your opinion of the Supreme Court ruling yesterday in the stop and frisk law?

A. I was very heartened to see that opinion, because I think sometimes we become so preoccupied with civil liberties as they affect the individual that we allow the general public—the great mass of law-abiding people—to be put in an untenable position by our adherence to the exact letter of every constitutional safeguard of a personal right. I think certainly with the amount of lawlessness that there is on the streets today and with our desire to cut down crime, that this is a very effective weapon for the police to have. The average citizen may well resent the intrusion on his privacy [but] if he's of good motives, I'm sure he will realize that this is for his protection as an individual and not for his embarrassment.

Press conference
June 11, 1968

Willingness to tolerate individual irresponsibility under any circumstances other than insanity can crumble the walls of a constitutional democracy.

In excusing individual responsibility we condone lawlessness and encourage cynical leaders to exploit the madness of the mob.

July 30, 1968

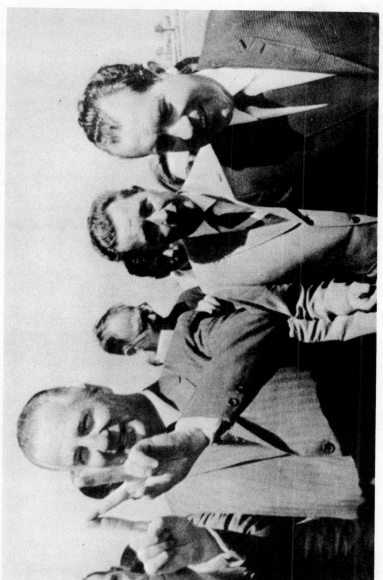

Student Unrest

Students always have objections to the way colleges are run. I doubt if we'll ever change that. Our problem is to make certain that we properly assess their objections and make changes where they are indicated, but don't overreact.

Press conference
March 28, 1968

I am pleased to see so many of the Greek Orthodox Church's young leaders here tonight. In an era when America's youth is characterized as being long on hair but lean on faith, it is reassuring to see so many determined to make their faith a vital force. With so much attention focused upon a minority of alienated young people, it is gratifying to realize that involved youth remain the majority. With all the notoriety given to those "dropping out" of society, we can solemnly thank God that many more are equally dedicated to changing society by "dropping in.". . . Nothing can be gained from without.

Address to the Seventeenth International Conference
of the Greek Orthodox Youth of America
New York City
July 30, 1968

Today's events at Bowie State College should amply demonstrate that this administration has no intention of yielding to the demands and threats of those who would take matters in their own hands and attempt to run the state government.

It is unfortunate that students, who no doubt have legitimate grievances, came under the spell of outside agitators and

112

sought to redress these grievances through occupation of the college administration building and denial of access to the campus, even to the college president. This was an intolerable situation—to the college administration, to the Board of Trustees, and to me. I am glad that it has been relieved without the use of force. But force was present in the state police that I sent to the campus today, and force would have been used had the need arisen.

Press statement
March 30, 1968

When people embark upon a course of action that's deliberately calculated to inflame and provoke other action in response to it, there's no end to how far they can go. And I don't feel, in my position, having the responsibility in this state to protect the public property and the public health, safety and welfare, I don't feel disposed to see some drastic thing happen at that college campus [Bowie State College, which Governor Agnew ordered temporarily closed] tonight and then have people ask me tomorrow: "Why didn't you take action to secure it?"

Press conference
April 4, 1968

When I heard there was unrest on the campus of Maryland State College I immediately decided to ask the students themselves to come to Annapolis at my invitation to discuss some of the problems with me. We've just concluded what I consider to be one of the most productive meetings that I've ever been in, and I want to say this: that at a time when most of us have been so terribly concerned about the violence . . . on college campuses, in one short meeting my faith in the young people of this country has been restored. My confidence has been heightened to a degree I didn't believe possible. And I find myself with a tremendous desire to work for

114

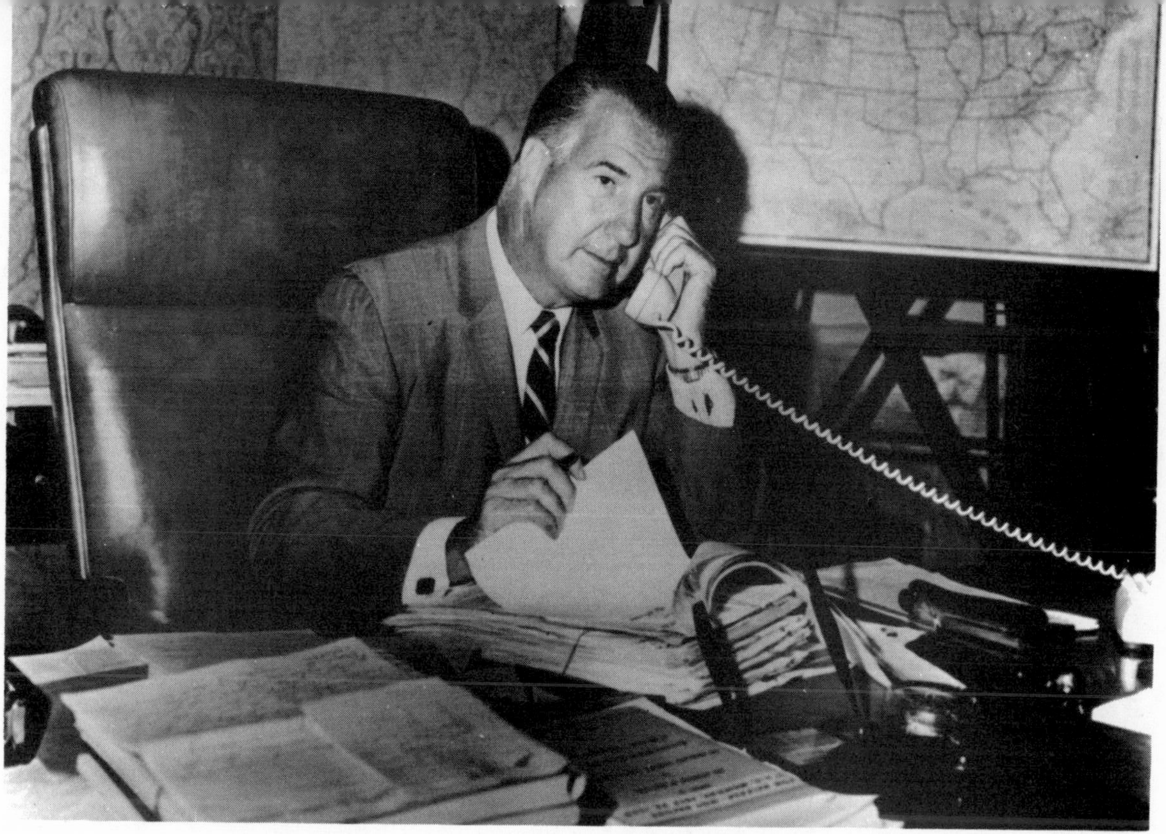

Wide World

these legitimate objectives that these students have put forward to me. . . .

The most important thing that these students did for me today was to believe me. And this is an exception . . . when you're in public office dealing with problems of unrest on the campus. We have agreed to form a joint committee consisting of a few students and a few members of my staff, and they will start tomorrow to try to reach solutions to these problems. . . .

I want to emphasize the difference between this approach and that which took place at Bowie State College. I think this is important. There has been no violence, no breaking of the law. There has been no beligerent conduct on the part of these students. They have been most mature in their approach. . . .

Annapolis
May 21, 1968

I've had many discussions with student leaders—some very recently—and one of the things I point out to them very graphically is that—don't expect me to agree with the fact that the establishment should be shot down. After all, I'm part of it. And don't think your desire to shoot it down is anything original because it's been going on for generations. And also, bear in mind that while you can contribute to the decision-making in a very positive way, the decision-making in the ultimate sense will only utilize your opinions as youth as one facet. Youth lacks, to some extent, experience. . . . On the other hand, it's unfettered by not being hidebound and following blindly into a course that just became comfortable through continued use. We've got to involve the young people. We've got to utilize their thinking. We've got to set the vitality and force of them moving in constructive ways to solve the problems.

Interview with the New York Times
August 25, 1968